DISINHERITED

How Washington
Is Betraying America's Young

DISINHERITED

How Washington
Is Betraying America's Young

Diana Furchtgott-Roth
and
Jared Meyer

ENCOUNTER BOOKS
New York • London

First American edition published in 2015 by Encounter Books,
an activity of Encounter for Culture and Education, Inc.,
a nonprofit, tax exempt corporation.
Encounter Books website address: www.encounterbooks.com

Manufactured in the United States and printed on
acid-free paper. The paper used in this publication meets
the minimum requirements of ANSI/NISO Z39.48-1992
(R 1997) (*Permanence of Paper*).

FIRST AMERICAN EDITION

LIBRARY OF CONGRESS CATALOGING-IN-PUBLICATION DATA
Furchtgott-Roth, Diana.
Disinherited : how Washington is betraying America's young / Diana Furchtgott-Roth , Jared
Meyer.
pages cm
Includes bibliographical references and index.
ISBN 978-1-59403-809-9 (hardback) — ISBN 978-1-59403-810-5 (ebook)
1. Generation Y—United States. 2. Age discrimination—United States. 3. Intergenerational
relations—United States. 4. United States—Economic conditions—21st century. I. Meyer,
Jared. II. Title.
HQ799.7.F87 2015
305.2—dc23
2014037248

To my millennials—Leon, Deborah, Francesca, Jeremy,
Chani, Godfrey, Theodore, and Richard
—D.F.R.

To my grandparents—Belva and Tom Kane,
and August and Barbara Meyer
—J.M.

TABLE OF CONTENTS

GLOSSARY

AARP – American Association of Retired Persons
ACA – Affordable Care Act
ACT – American College Testing
AFT – American Federation of Teachers
BLS – Bureau of Labor Statistics
CBO – Congressional Budget Office
CEO – chief executive officer
EMT – emergency medical technician
ESA – education savings accounts
GDP – gross domestic product
GPA – grade point average
HI – hospital insurance
MOOC – massive open online course
NCAA – National Collegiate Athletic Association
NEA – National Education Association
NOC – Neighborhood Outreach Connection
OASDI – Old Age, Survivors, and Disability Insurance Program
OECD – Organisation of Economic Cooperation and Development
PISA – Programme for International Student Assessment
P.S. – public school
ROC – Restaurant Opportunities Center United
SMI – supplementary medical insurance
STEM – science, technology, engineering, and mathematics
UFCW – United Food and Commercial Workers International Union

INTRODUCTION AND SUMMARY:
THE OVERARCHING PROBLEM

In a speech to high school graduates in Topeka, Kansas, in May 2014, First Lady Michelle Obama told the assembled students: "I am so proud of all that you've accomplished.... And I cannot wait to see everything you will achieve in the years ahead."

But these days many Americans born between the early 1980s and the beginning of the 21st century, often called "millennials" or "Generation Y," have not seen success. For them, achieving success will be more difficult than it was for young people in the past.

This is the first generation of young Americans that our government systematically disfavors and the first generation of Americans whose prospects are lower than those of their parents. They have been disinherited from their birthright.

Many older Americans think that they are disadvantaged by today's culture or by old age in general. Claire Sommers, in her eighties and living in Brooklyn, finds it hard, for instance, to use modern technology such as computers and smartphones. Her husband, Sonny, finds it increasingly difficult to complete daily tasks around the house.

But in terms of government spending, Claire and Sonny are winners—unintended winners, because they never wanted to take advantage of their grandchildren, but winners nevertheless. Washington politicians increase the federal debt with unfunded promises to retirees, and, if Claire and Sonny's grandchildren get jobs and pay taxes, they are the ones who will end up funding that debt.

Over five years into the economic recovery, the unemployment rate for young people ages 20 to 24 is 11 percent overall and 20 percent for African Americans. The teenage unemployment rate is at 20 percent, and the African-American teen unemployment rate is at 33 percent.[1]

Job creation is proceeding slowly, but the largest share of gains is going to Americans ages 55 and older. Young adults have hardly benefited from declines in the unemployment rate. Many, discouraged, have given up on finding work and are leaving the labor force. The percentage of teens and young people employed or looking for work, known as the labor-force participation rate, is at the lowest level since the government began keeping records on this in 1948. In contrast, Americans 55 and older are working in increasing numbers and now have the highest labor-force participation rate since the early 1960s.[2] Since the late 1990s, the labor-force participation rates of workers 65 and older have been rising steadily as well.

These trends of increased labor-force participation by older workers are commendable—after all, life expectancy continues to lengthen. What is troubling is that the biggest decline in labor-force participation is among workers ages 16 to 24, from a rate of 61 percent in 2004 to 55 percent in 2014. In other words, young people have been hit the hardest by the recession and slow economic recovery.

Male Employment Population Ratio, by Age

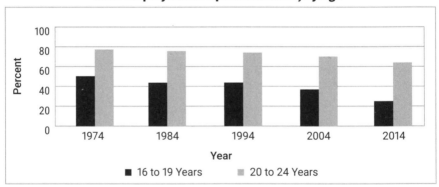

Source: Bureau of Labor Statistics, Current Population Survey

This is causing millennials to delay important milestones in their lives, such as getting a full-time job, moving out of the family home, and buying a house. More are working part time, because that is all the work that they can find.

The percentage of employed 20- to 24-year-olds who work part time was 21 percent in the mid-1980s. This percentage grew steadily to 30 percent by 2008 and then rose to 36 percent in 2014—an increase of more than 70 percent in just a quarter century. The percentage of employed people over the age of 25 who work part time increased only 11 percent over that same time period.[3]

Those unable to find jobs find it difficult to pay rent or qualify for a mortgage. From 1968 to 2007, the percentage of 18- to 31-year-olds living with their parents held steady at around 32 percent. By 2012, that number had increased to 36 percent. Among young people 18 to 24 years old, 56 percent lived at home in 2012—a historic high.[4] "The unwritten social contract of their [parents of millennials] era presumed that the economy would be strong enough so that when children reached a certain age, they could be 'launched' into the adult world and would not crash. It's this contract that has now broken down," explains columnist Robert Samuelson.[5] Only one-third of 27-year-olds, those who graduated college during the recession, are married.[6] Starting a family is much more difficult while struggling to find work.

Percent of 18- to 31-Year-Olds Living at Home

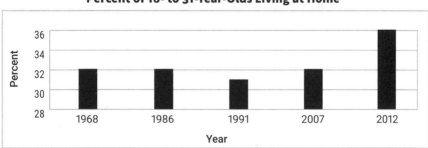

Source: Pew Research Center tabulations of March 2012 Current Population Survey data

Each section of this book is able to stand on its own. Readers may find some chapters more interesting than others and can follow their own progression while reading the book. We interviewed a number of people in the course of our research. Some were glad to speak on the record, and we have provided their full names. Others preferred to be anonymous, and when quoting them or discussing their experiences, we use only their first names or a pseudonym. The book is divided as follows:

Part I: Stealing from the Young to Enrich the Old describes Washington's expansion of entitlement benefits and other government services, along with the taxes young people will have to pay to support them, mostly to subsidize older Americans. The federal government has a debt of

$18 trillion, and this is only projected to rise.[7] Entitlement programs such as Social Security and Medicare are bankrupt. Unfunded liabilities driven by these programs push the total federal fiscal shortfall to more than $200 trillion. When Social Security and Medicare were originally put in place, no one forecast that they would grow so rapidly and take over almost two-thirds of the federal budget. In addition, state governments face $5 trillion in unfunded liabilities, mostly in retirement-benefit debt.[8]

In **Chapter 1: Unfunded Promises**, we describe how politicians in Washington are taking from the future earnings of young people, many of them not old enough to vote, to pay for services for their parents and grandparents, who do vote. Burdened with an obligation to pay government debt they did not incur, young people begin life at least partially robbed of their birthright.

Their parents and grandparents, beneficiaries of the New Deal and Great Society programs that are now bankrupting America, never intended this. They are deeply concerned that their children and grandchildren cannot find jobs and are facing a future of decreased opportunity. They never anticipated that their comforts would come at the expense of their progeny. But, regardless of intentions, that is what has occurred. The question remains, What can be done to create a system that is more fair and sustainable?

Mary Parrilli, now in her twenties, living outside Chicago, told us: "I am outraged. We have been scammed, end of story. I do not expect to get back any of the money I am paying into Social Security—to me, it's just another tax. I think people should help the elderly, especially their own family, but it is immoral for the government to force this upon us. This is a perfect example of punishing the young and successful, and rewarding the irresponsible."

We know the increasingly devastating fiscal condition being handed to our nation's youth. Every Social Security and Medicare Trustees Report and every Budget Outlook from the nonpartisan Congressional Budget Office shows fiscal deficits far into the future. These deficits drive the national debt even higher, and someday the bill will come due. Only substantial tax increases or spending cuts will solve the problem, and, judging by the current political climate, these are not coming anytime soon.

Our budget is controlled by "dead men ruling," in the words of economist Eugene Steuerle. "In 2009," he writes, "every dollar of revenue had been committed before that Congress walked in the doors of the Capitol."[9] Because of automatic entitlement spending, Congress is unable to balance the budget without taking direct action to rein in the growth of these programs. To make matters worse, spending in 2009 was $3.5 trillion and revenue was $2.1 trillion, leaving a deficit of $1.4 trillion.[10] Seven years from now, the deficit is expected to surpass $1 trillion again and continue rising after that. This will leave debt held by the public at more than 79 percent of GDP in 2024, compared with about 73 percent now.[11] While this disproportionate spending is clearly a major component of the future problems facing America's youth, the issue extends far beyond the fact that young people will be stuck with their parents' and grandparents' debt.

As if this were not enough, the Affordable Care Act has raised health-insurance premiums for young Americans and lowered them for middle-aged and older people. Young, healthy Americans are, in effect, being required to pay for the health care of older Americans. We address this in **Chapter 2: Paying for Parents' Health Care**. Rather than solve the problem, Washington has added to it by raising the cost of insurance for millennials and lowering it for their parents.

We interviewed Tommy Groves (not his real name), a young professional working at a small firm in Washington, D.C., whose health-insurance provider terminated his coverage. Tommy's employer gave him a set amount of money to spend on health insurance, and he spent hours on the computer trying to purchase insurance through the D.C. health exchange, called D.C. Health Link. When that failed, he spent hours on the phone. Even that was not sufficient to allow him to enroll, so he had to visit the office to sign up in person. Tommy's premium for his "silver plan" went up to $225 a month from his $175 pre-ACA rate.

Before the passage of the Affordable Care Act, premiums for 18-year-olds cost about one-fifth those of 64-year-olds.[12] Since older people are at a much greater risk of serious health problems than are people just out of high school, it makes sense that insurance companies would charge the 64-year-old more. Given that income typically rises with age, the 64-year-old would be better able to afford the higher premiums. But the new law prohibits insurance companies from charging older people more than three times as much as it charges young Americans, so premiums for people such as Tommy had to increase.

Part II: Keeping Young People Uneducated describes educational barriers to progress. Young people are disadvantaged from their elementary and high school years until they graduate from college—and beyond. In elementary and secondary school, ill-qualified teachers are protected from being fired. This favors older teachers, but it harms young teachers and the students who would benefit from high-quality teachers.

In their college years, young people are encouraged to attend a four-year university, even if doing so is not the right choice for them. The current system of federal student aid raises the cost of college tuition, so students are forced to take on debt that will burden them for many years after they graduate. We need to encourage innovation in the classroom at all levels of learning, whether through charter schools, voucher programs, or massive open online courses to reverse the trend of declining educational performance.

The betrayal of America's young begins with America's primary-education system. In **Chapter 3: The Failure of Primary and Secondary Education**, we show that states do not require children to pass content-based exams to progress to the next grade, so children are often shuffled from one grade to the next on the basis of attendance, even if they do not know the material.

Maybe states do not apply educational standards because many students would be hard-pressed to meet them. Once the envy of the world, America's primary-education system has deteriorated. With the rest of the world catching up to or pulling ahead of the United States in educational achievement, failing to prepare students for an increasingly globalized economy is the height of unfairness.

Nowadays, many public schools are run for the benefit of their employees rather than their students. Compounding the lack of achievement are teachers' unions that stubbornly resist commonsense educational improvements, such as charter schools and voucher programs. When it comes to delaying school openings from 7:15 a.m. to a time more suitable to teenagers' well-known sleep schedules, school boards resist change in order to maintain a status quo that public-sector unions support. Unfortunately, many local governments choose to protect union interests over their students' futures.

Some families can manage to send their children to private schools, and others can afford to move to better school districts. But many millennials are doomed by a failed public school system that cannot meet the demands of a 21st-century economy.

After students graduate from high school, the betrayal continues. In **Chapter 4: Drowning in College Debt,** we show that more than 7 in 10 college students take out loans to finance college, and the average amount of student loan debt is $29,400.[13] But many students graduate with little hope of finding a job, left with nothing but a mountain of debt to repay. William Bennett, secretary of education from 1985 to 1988, has shown how "politically charged pseudo learning" has diminished the value of a college degree, while government financial-aid programs have pushed the cost of college tuition sky-high.

Even though the return from a two-year community-college education in a generally well-paid field, such as health-care services or computer programming, can be greater for the individual than the return from a four-year college degree, many high school guidance counselors do not recommend community college. College-trained with bachelor's degrees themselves, they look down on community colleges or worry that they will be penalized for recommending two-year institutions to low-performing students. Instead, they shovel entire classes into four-year colleges, ignoring the looming high level of debt at the end of the process.

Connor Wolf, a young political reporter, sat down with us to talk about college debt and the state of higher education in America. "Most if not all decisions in life should be based on a cost-benefit analysis," he said. "This is especially true for major financial decisions like college." While this point might seem obvious, most people do not approach higher education with this mind-set.

What Connor told us next was surprising. Even though he said his college experience was superb, he has some reservations: "If I were to look at it now, I would say beyond a doubt that the benefits I received from going to college didn't come close to the price of that experience, and, from what I understand, many students and recent graduates feel the same way."

Connor also described the frustration and pressure he felt while trying to find a job after college graduation. "I imagine that trying to find a job is unnerving in any circumstance when a person is young and competing against people with much more experience, but with a bad economy and a lack of available jobs, it only becomes more frightening," he said. "After graduation, I looked for any job, from an entry-level position where I could start building a career to a basic restaurant job so I would be slightly less broke. There was nothing available. Finally, after four months, I found a catering job that provided me with enough money to afford to start some internships related to my career interests. I didn't get a college-level job until a year and a half after graduating, yet I consider myself lucky because many recent graduates are still struggling. It really is unacceptable." As Connor's comments make clear, America has failed, and is failing, to properly educate its young.

The next step in our betrayal of millennials is in the workplace. **Part III: Regulations That Cripple the Young** shows how Washington and state governments prevent young people from entering the job market. This is done in multiple ways. Occupational licensing requirements are meant to protect public safety, but they instead protect established businesses and workers at the expense of everyday consumers, entrepreneurs, and young workers; and they make many promising career paths prohibitively expensive or time-consuming to enter.

Minimum-wage laws, though well-intentioned, make it more difficult for the young and low-skilled to acquire valuable work experience. Unpaid internships, which teach the hard and soft skills necessary for future success, are limited. Again, the government is telling young people that they are not free to work. We need to roll back these destructive labor-market laws at every level of government so the first step on the career ladder can be within reach for all young people.

Washington should do as much as possible to ensure that young people—who have large debts to pay off, including outstanding college loans, and little to show in the way of education—can get a job and start earning income. But the reverse is true. In **Chapter 5: Licensing Requirements Keep Out the Young**, we describe how occupational licenses restrict millennials' ability to start their own businesses. Occupational licensing is an often-overlooked but substantial barrier to the workforce, and it extends far beyond doctors and lawyers. Countless occupations—from manicurists to door-repair contractors to auctioneers—require a license from the government in order to work. Over the course of a career, 4 in 10 Americans will need to obtain the government's permission to work.

Despite the claims of proponents, these occupational licenses do little to protect public safety. Rather, they protect those who are already established in their careers from the competition young workers would generate. Interior designers, though licensed in only three states and the District of Columbia, need an average of six years of training to work, but who has died from clashing drapes? In contrast, emergency medical technicians who hold lives in their hands need only 33 days of training.[14]

Occupational licensing has a disproportionately negative effect on young people looking to start their careers. Paths to entrepreneurship are cut off, not only for them but also for older workers looking to start small businesses. This further limits the creation of local jobs that open opportunities for young people. Today's occupational licensing policies bring back memories of medieval regulations aimed at protecting established tradesmen at the expense of potential competitors. In the Middle Ages, tradesmen formed guilds to lock out newcomers. Today, all levels of government implement policies that protect established, politically connected workers. This keeps young people from fully participating in the workforce and following their career dreams.

Occupational licensing is not the only factor in preventing young people from working. **Chapter 6: Banned from the Job Market** describes the high minimum wages that keep younger millennials out of work. Similarly, once commonplace, unpaid internships in for-profit companies are now disallowed out of concern that companies might use them to exploit the interns.

University of California economist David Neumark has shown that young workers with low skills are harmed the most by the minimum wage. This is not surprising given that half of minimum-wage earners are between the ages of 16 and 24.[15] If people cannot get their first job, how can they get their second or third? People who take minimum-wage jobs gain entry into the professional world. Once they are in, they can keep rising.

When the minimum wage is set above someone's skill level, that person is left on the sidelines. Businesses are not forced to pay the minimum wage, because they always have the option to not hire people at all. If the minimum wage rises too high, employers have an incentive to replace their less-skilled workers with more-skilled ones or with machines. The first rung of the career ladder remains out of reach when the minimum wage is too high, and this has far-reaching effects later in young people's lives.

While the minimum wage has been politicized, its negative consequences should concern people across the political spectrum. Linda Mack, owner of a bike store in Silver Spring, Maryland, is a liberal Democrat. Yet when her county voted to raise the minimum wage in three increments to $11.25 an hour, she foresaw problems for her business and for the young people she trains. "I want to teach people how to work and hold down a job," Linda told us. "I agree that competent people should all be making $11.25 an hour. But when I bring new people in and attempt to train them, there is a reverse cash flow. My newest people are a drain on my staff and our cash. They are effectively useless for months."

She continued: "I start people at $8.00 an hour. So the summer help that we must bring in would bleed the business dry at $11.25 an hour, in that they really can't do much their first summer other than say hello and point to the bike pumps so visiting cyclists can pump up their bikes. In year two, they are usually worth that $11.25 or more, or I don't bring them back. The cost of bringing new workers into the workforce falls more heavily on my shoulders than ever before. I am going to have to raise prices to cover this social good, training young people to think and work."

Linda had a well-educated, intelligent young woman working for her. Her biggest challenges were learning to come to work every day, do her job competently, present herself professionally, and understand that failing to show up caused hardship for her colleagues. Some might think that these skills are just common sense, but many people have to learn them.

Linda does not know what the solution is. "I think that I've been effective in training young people, on my little micro scale. But I do think an $11.25 minimum wage is going to cause a big adjustment in the cost of services and goods, create an even bigger underclass of unemployable people, and cause some fairly drastic changes at my small bike shop."

Prohibitions against unpaid internships harm the very people they are supposed to protect. Just as with increases in the minimum wage, businesses are less likely to invest in training young people in the hard and soft skills necessary for a career if they have to pay a high cost for the training. Firms from Condé Nast to Fox Searchlight have discontinued their internship programs. It would be far better to view internships as education that comes with the added benefit of real-world experience.

Laws that discourage young people from finding work make it harder for them to gain crucial career experience. This lack of early workplace exposure can have profound social and economic consequences later in life.

Our solutions and conclusion are presented in **Part IV: Where To from Here?** In **Chapter 7: Reclaiming the Disinherited Generation**, we describe solutions to ballooning entitlement spending, ineffective education systems, and workplace constraints, which all combine to create an environment that systematically imperils young people's futures. Those with access to a good education and a broad network of connections will continue to do well. But what about those who are kept from succeeding in school and are not blessed with professional connections? What will happen to them?

Some, such as *New York Times* columnist Paul Krugman, think that the solution is more government spending and higher taxes. As he sees it, deregulation is the root of the problem. If government were larger and gave more handouts, and taxes were raised to fund these goodies, then young people would do better. Extensive data from European economies show that this argument does not hold water. Countries in Europe have higher taxes, free or subsidized education, heavily subsidized health care, and ample leave for vacation, illness, and childbirth. Yet youth unemployment is even higher in Europe than in America. The unemployment rates for Greek and Spanish youth hover above 50 percent, and the average for the European Union is close to 25 percent.[16]

In **Chapter 8: Conclusion**, we show how politicians in both parties are responsible for the betrayal of America's young. Partisan talking points are not enough to end this outrage—all these destructive policies began long before the current administration. While the problem is bipartisan in nature, the solution is, too. Putting an end to that which disadvantages America's youth should be a major concern for people all across the political spectrum. The time has come to recognize that holding back a nation's youth is the antithesis of fairness and no way to make economic or social progress.

While conversation about any aspect of the systematic betrayal of America's young is useful, we focus on the three major policy failures—ballooning government spending, ineffective education systems, and workplace regulation—that combine to create an environment that places young people at a disadvantage. This betrayal is not intentional. In this book we lay out the scope of the problem and what will be necessary to solve it.

Plainly stated, Washington is robbing America's young. Our country is facing a crisis, and change is essential in order for young people to achieve the future they deserve.

PART I

STEALING FROM THE YOUNG TO ENRICH THE OLD

America's national debt is $18 trillion and climbing. Social Security and Medicare, mammoth programs that provide generous benefits to seniors, consume 40 cents of every dollar spent by the federal government, a proportion expected to increase. When future spending obligations are stacked up against expected tax receipts, America owes $205 trillion—more than 12 times our GDP—a figure that dwarfs the oft-cited $18 trillion number.

Today's young people will pay the bills when they inevitably come due, while today's seniors enjoy a comfortable retirement. Working people contribute 15.3 percent of their paychecks to payroll taxes that only partially fund these programs. If Washington does not act to reform entitlements, it will mean either a much higher tax bill for millennials or a steep reduction in benefits.

At the state level, runaway pension plans for public-sector employees pose a serious threat to state budgets. As well-connected public-sector unions fight against any changes to generous pensions, it is the poorly represented taxpayers, the young people just starting their careers or those who cannot yet vote, who will end up footing the bill.

Taxes and unfunded deficits are just one side of the story. Government programs such as the Affordable Care Act rob the young in other ways. Young people, especially young men, have seen their health-insurance premiums soar under the new health-care law. Regulations that artificially hold down the premiums of their parents leave young people to pick up the slack.

New mandates on the labor market will also harm young people when they take effect. In 2016, small businesses that do not offer health insurance as a benefit will need to pay the post-tax equivalent of $60,000 in fines to hire a 50th full-time worker. This will slow the growth of hiring and discourage millennials from seeking a job. Youth labor-force participation in America is already at historic lows—only 55 percent of young people are in the workforce.

While many government programs—Social Security, Medicare, the Affordable Care Act—have the admirable goal of caring for the elderly or helping the uninsured, they also have unintended consequences. The unseen losers, those who silently shoulder the costs of these programs, are America's young. The following section explains how government steals from the young to enrich the old—and how we can redesign policies and programs to work for everyone.

CHAPTER 1

UNFUNDED PROMISES

Jared's grandfather, August Meyer, an octogenarian living in Minnesota, does not see his Social Security checks as entitlements because he paid Social Security taxes during his entire career as an airline-engine shop foreman. He was told that the Social Security system would invest his hard-earned money and use the returns to ensure that he had a comfortable retirement. But owing to a series of botched and unfunded promises, Social Security has turned into a pay-as-you-go system in which the money he paid in, as payroll taxes taken out of each paycheck, was spent long ago and the money young people are now paying goes directly to retirees in his position.

In terms of government spending, August is a winner. He is an unintended winner, because he never wanted to take advantage of his grandchildren, but he is a winner nevertheless. The government increases the federal debt, and, if August's grandchildren get jobs and pay taxes, they are the ones who will be stuck paying it back. Our government requires young people to pay an outsize share of taxes, loans, and health-insurance premiums—all to benefit older Americans. This system is neither sustainable nor fair.

Jean Thompson (not her real name), a young professional, agrees. "I think my generation is paying for the boomers' credit cards with the entitlement programs [Social Security, Medicare, and now Obamacare] as they are structured now," she told us. "I remember reading in *U.S. News and World Report* that the interest from these programs and the national debt will absorb 92 cents of every dollar in the next 10 years.

Boomers have less in personal savings as compared with other generational cohorts, and I suspect that this is in part because they are relying on these programs they believe they have paid in to, even if Social Security and other programs aren't exactly paid for in this manner."

Jean studied demography, so she approaches these problems in demographic terms. She is mildly forgiving of the boomers, because she does not think they understood that fertility rates were declining. In the 1970s, as these entitlement programs were gathering steam, people were concerned about a population bomb, not a birth dearth. But with declining fertility rates, sustaining entitlement programs is difficult unless the American economy is exceptionally strong. There are fewer young people, so they will have to contribute more to the system, as a group through a high labor-force participation rate and individually through ever-higher payroll taxes. Economic growth has been tepid since the recession, though, so young people lack financial resources.

Jean sees that Washington has been reluctant to fix this system, all while the federal deficit grows. Politicians have not acknowledged how much this system hurts young people. It is tough for older Americans to understand why young people might live at home with their parents, carry large debt loads, or have trouble finding work. And because older Americans are a large voting bloc, politicians have resisted increasing the amount of money that older people pay to the entitlement programs they benefit from.

Few young people know that America is $18 trillion in debt, and fewer know that this is only the *federal* debt. Of this amount, $5 trillion is held by the government and $13 trillion is privately held.[1] Social Security contributed $69 billion toward the debt, but that is just the tip of the iceberg.[2] When future spending obligations on entitlements are compared with future tax obligations, the so-called fiscal gap is $205 trillion.[3] This is 12 times GDP and 16 times official debt held by the public. In simpler terms, we are broke.

In addition, states have their own deficits, which will have to be funded by young Americans. States are $5 trillion in debt from unfunded pension liabilities.[4]

"I think that our political institutions and political leaders have accommodated themselves to deficit spending and growing debt and acquired a stake in their continuance," Hudson Institute senior fellow Christopher DeMuth wrote in *National Review.* "Disagreements over the consequences and immediacy of the problem are always resolved in favor of borrowing more to address the problems of the moment and deferring 'debt consolidation' (through some combination of higher taxes, lower spending, and higher economic growth) to a later time. The American body politic has acquired deficit-attention disorder."[5]

Paying off the amount of the federal fiscal gap—irrespective of state deficits—would require an immediate and permanent 57 percent increase in all federal taxes. In 20 years, this amount becomes 69 percent and in 30 years, 76 percent. Another way to close the fiscal gap would be to institute immediate and permanent cuts of 37 percent in all federal spending except that which services the debt; in 20 years, this number becomes 43 percent, and in 30 years, it balloons to 46 percent.[6] Neither of these options is politically feasible, but the consequences of delayed action only worsen as time passes.

This leaves young Americans with two options. They can either pay substantially higher taxes than their parents do, while not receiving any more benefits, or they can pay the same rate as their elders and receive far fewer benefits. Both outcomes are grossly unfair. "You have been conscripted to finance other people's retirement and health-care needs, regardless of what impact this will have on your life. Your duty is to set aside your own happiness in order to serve the needs of the old," Don Watkins explains to millennials in his book *Rooseveltcare.*[7]

The Congressional Budget Office estimates that if the country continues on its current path, the federal deficit will be $7.2 trillion aggregated over the next 10 years. CBO's job is to analyze the effect that current laws on spending and taxes will have over the next decade. Based on their assessment, they construct projections of deficits or surpluses. These days, deficits are all they see, and these are getting larger. CBO has projected that government revenues, nearly all of which come from taxes, will stay around 18 percent of GDP until 2024, while spending would rise from slightly more than 20 percent of GDP to 22 percent of GDP over the same 10-year period.[8]

Real Federal Debt per Capita

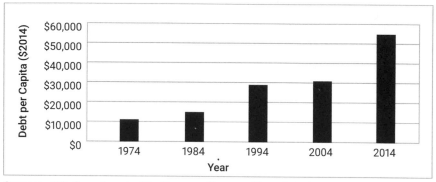

Sources: U.S. Department of the Treasury, Treasury Direct; U.S. Census Bureau, Population Estimates; and Bureau of Labor Statistics, Consumer Price Index

Federal Debt to GDP

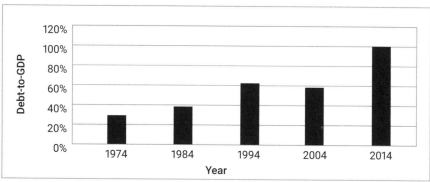

Sources: U.S. Department of the Treasury, Treasury Direct; Bureau of Economic Analysis, National Income and Product Accounts

It is not just that young people are paying for their elders' entitlement programs, but that those currently in Washington are handicapped by decisions made by previous administrations. Federal spending in 2014 on mandatory programs such as entitlements equaled 12 percent of GDP, whereas discretionary spending was 7 percent of GDP.[9] This leaves less money for more-essential functions of government such as building and maintaining America's transportation infrastructure.

This is not to say that Washington is starved for funding. Federal debt from government activities outside these major entitlement programs is also projected to rise over the next decade.

In *Dead Men Ruling: How to Restore Fiscal Freedom and Rescue Our Future*, Urban Institute scholar Eugene Steuerle shows that the federal deficit is primarily driven by programs put in place long ago.[10] These programs were created and essentially set on autopilot. Since then, they have grown in scope and scale. Washington has not mustered the political will to end the entitlement programs it has inherited. Now the government finds itself unable to adapt to 21st-century challenges, as it is increasingly constrained by laws passed in the 20th century. Young Americans are funding Social Security and Medicare for the current population of elderly Americans, but the programs are scheduled to go bankrupt long before people who are young today reach retirement age.

If Washington does not change present law, the Social Security trust fund will be depleted by 2033.[11] This means that for people retiring in 20 years, those Social Security checks will not be paid in full. The Hospital Insurance component of Medicare is scheduled to exhaust its trust funds by 2030.[12] Recall the octogenarian August Meyer, who spent a large part of his career paying into Medicare and was confident he had earned every penny of his Social Security checks—but his two knee replacements are not cheap. As the costs of end-of-life care continue to balloon, it is clear that those in his situation are getting the best end of the deal.

When taken together, Social Security and Medicare account for almost 40 percent of the federal spending in 2014.[13] Even though Social Security and Medicare are on an unsustainable path, young people and their employers continue to pay a combined 15.3 percent of their paychecks into the programs, funding current retirees with contributions the young will probably never see paid back.[14]

The beginnings of Social Security go back to 1935, when the Social Security Act became law. While the Act was intended to provide for the needy and destitute, many prominent lawmakers raised substantive questions about its practicality, constitutionality, and potential for growth. Daniel Reed, then a New York Republican in the House, remarked that with the passage of the act, Americans would feel "the lash of the dictator."[15] Representative John Taber, another New York Republican, asserted, "Never in the history of the world has any measure been brought here so insidiously designed as to prevent business recovery, to enslave workers."[16] Senator Thomas Gore, an Oklahoma Democrat and the grandfather of author Gore Vidal, was quoted as saying, "Isn't this socialism?"[17]

Social Security had humble beginnings. In 1937, the program included a mere 53,236 beneficiaries who received a total of just $21 million in today's dollars.[18] Considering that the American government now spends $7 million a minute, this was not a substantial amount of money by today's standards.[19] By the end of 2013, total beneficiaries amounted to 58 million—over 1,000 times more beneficiaries than in 1937.[20] In fiscal year 2013, Social Security cost $808 billion—nearly 40,000 times what it cost in 1937, adjusted for inflation—amounting to almost 23 percent of federal spending.[21] According to the 2014 Social Security Trustees' Report, with an infinite horizon, the present value of unfunded liabilities in 2013 was $24.9 trillion.[22]

Social Security needs to move from a pay-as-you-go system, where what is paid in is quickly paid out, to a sustainable system that allows payments to grow as investments that can help pay for retirement. An adjustment in benefit calculations, sooner rather than later, will go a long way toward shoring up Social Security's troubled finances. If the program is to be there for young people when they retire, something has to change—and fast.

Geoffrey Levesque, a recent college graduate who is trying to build a career in television production, resembles many of his peers in that he does not expect to ever receive the money back that he is now paying in to Social Security. "Already I don't know if the baby boomer generation will receive all of its Social Security," he told us. "So I can't even imagine what it will be for my generation. With how this government spends money, it will be unlikely. Whatever your political views are, there is a duty to help the elderly. They worked hard for their money. Still, I would be upset if I did not receive all of my Social Security, but, based on my experience so far, I am always prepared to be disappointed by the government."

Social Security is not the only major entitlement program that is facing serious actuarial problems. The projected aggregate cost of Medicare is staggering, and it is the main driver of our debt. The Congressional Budget Office has estimated that, under an extended baseline, Medicare expenditures as a percentage of GDP would grow from 3 percent today to 5.5 percent in 2050, and to 9.3 percent in 2089.[23]

Medicare's modest origins can be traced to 1965, when President Lyndon Johnson signed it into law. The program was designed to provide medical care for those 65 and older, at a time when life expectancy was about 70 years.[24] In 1966, 19 million people signed up for the program, and it cost $30 billion in today's dollars.[25] By 2013, 52 million people were enrolled—nearly a threefold increase. The program cost $583 billion in fiscal year 2013—20 times higher than costs in 1966—which represented 14 percent of total federal outlays that year.[26] To understand just how much the program has expanded in the last 30 years,[27] consider that as recently as 1980 Medicare spending amounted to a mere $101 billion, covering 28 million people.[28]

Medicare spending is projected to rise to 6.9 percent of GDP by 2088. Projected revenues—coming from payroll taxes and taxes on Old Age, Survivors, and Disability Insurance Program (OASDI) benefits that go into the Hospital Insurance (HI) trust fund—rise from 1.4 percent of GDP today to 1.8 percent of GDP by 2088, assuming current law. The portion of non-interest Medicare income that comes from taxes will drop from 41 percent to 28 percent at the same time that general revenue transfers will rise from 43 to 52 percent, and the share of premiums will rise from 14 to 18 percent.[29]

This change in the distribution of financing will happen because costs for Medicare Parts B and D (which are funded by general revenues) increase at a faster rate than do the Part A costs, according to Trustees' projections. In 2088, the Supplementary Medical Insurance (SMI) program will need general revenue transfers of 3.3 percent of GDP, and the HI deficit will reach 0.5 percent of GDP in 2088. No provision exists to finance this deficit through general revenue transfers or any other revenue source.[30]

The Medicare Modernization Act of 2003 requires that the Boards of Trustees determine each year whether the annual deficit exceeds 45 percent of total Medicare costs in any of the first seven fiscal years of the 75-year projection period. If it does exceed 45 percent, then they must include a report on "excess general-revenue Medicare funding." If two of these reports are required consecutively, then there is a "Medicare funding warning" that forces the president to respond to the overrun by proposing legislation within 15 days of the next budget submission. Congress is then required to consider the proposal with priority. So far, Washington has not responded to the funding warnings that have been a part of seven of the last eight reports. Politicians are breaking their own law. Again, Washington does nothing and then wonders why our fiscal position is deteriorating.

Washington did pass a law constraining Medicare's growth. Reimbursements to Medicare physicians are supposed to be trimmed whenever Medicare exceeds a pre-set growth rate. But Washington repeatedly repeals the proposed cuts to Medicare physicians. If it failed to do so, no doctor would participate in Medicare.

In 2014, the HI deficit was $15 billion. Until 2030, interest earnings and asset redemptions will cover deficits of the HI trust fund. At that time, the trust fund will be bankrupt. After that, new revenue will be necessary. This will require some combination of increasing taxes, reducing benefits, cutting other government spending, and borrowing more from taxpayers. If nothing is done, then borrowing from taxpayers will need to reach 4.4 percent of GDP by 2040.[31]

As these programs balloon, the old gain, and the young pay. Adjustments to Medicare's growth rate, both in terms of coverage and cost, need to be seriously evaluated if the program is going to remain viable for those who are paying for it.

The Social Security and Medicare Trustees' report highlights the commonly known problems with Social Security. In 2013, Social Security benefits cost 14 percent of taxable payrolls. By 2035, they are projected to cost 17 percent; they will climb upward to 18 percent in 2088. For Medicare, costs were at 4 percent of taxable payrolls in 2013 and are projected to climb to 5 percent by 2050, then up to 6 percent in 2088.[32]

If trends continue, workers could be paying a combined employer-employee payroll tax rate of 32 percent in 2050 just to cover Medicare and Social Security payments.[33] The rate paid now is 15 percent.[34] That is a major cut to take-home pay that will severely affect consumer spending and investment. A 32 percent payroll tax rate seems unimaginable in 2014, but it is below rates paid by some other major industrialized countries. In France, the rate is 42 percent; in Germany, it is 39 percent; in Italy, 40 percent; and in Spain, 37 percent. The United Kingdom has one of the lower rates in Europe, at 24 percent.[35]

That does not even count the amount that taxpayers will have to pay from their paychecks for state deficits. States hold an additional $5 trillion in liability, of which $4.4 trillion represents debt for pensions and other post-employment benefits. This does not even include the pension or capital-market debt of cities, counties, and other local government entities. A true picture of America's fiscal position should include all levels of government liabilities.

To cover the total unfunded pension liabilities of state governments, each person in the United States would have to pay $15,052.[36] But there is a vast spread between states. Tennessee is in the best financial shape, with $6,531 per person in liabilities. It is followed by Wisconsin, at $6,720; and Indiana, at $7,304. Alaska is in the worst shape, with $40,639 per person. In the continental United States, the state in the worst shape is Illinois, at $25,740; followed by Ohio, at $25,028; and Connecticut, at $24,080. Both red and blue states face towering unfunded promises because the defined-benefit pension system allows politicians from all parties to grant something for nothing—and to defer the inevitable bill.

During economic booms, states deliver more-generous pensions to their employees, but during economic downturns, these increases are rarely pared back. This means that states make promises to public-sector unions that they usually cannot afford.

Absent major concessions, these pensions will have to be paid over time to the 19 million men and women who work for state, county, municipal, or school-district government. If pension-fund income is insufficient to cover these obligations, as is expected, the burden will shift further to state taxpayers. If Washington decides to bail out the states, all American taxpayers, no matter how young, will be liable for these irresponsible promises.

This dire debt has arisen even though the National Association of State Budget Officers found that 49 states had balanced-budget requirements in 2008. Forty-four states require the governor to submit a balanced budget, 41 require the legislature to pass a balanced budget, 37 require the governor to sign a balanced budget, and 43 prevent the state from carrying over a deficit.[37]

How has this happened? Even when there are balanced-budget amendments, states are often free to use different funds that are not required to be in balance. The balanced-budget requirements typically apply only to general fund budgets. This leaves large amounts of revenues and expenditures free from budget constraints.

Many states can also issue debt to balance their budgets. It is not surprising that, just like the federal government, state governments pass their bills to future generations. Cash-based accounting schemes allow states to issue debt as a way around balanced-budget requirements. Loan proceeds are counted as revenues under cash-based accounting. Even though loans have to be paid back, states can meet their budget requirements by not counting debt due in the future and by shifting expenses from one year to another. Under cash accounting, if a state owes $10 million in annual pension contributions but puts in only $5 million, the budget is still considered "balanced." All this does is postpone the payment of the debt. This is why cash-based accounting is not a widely accepted method for businesses. The Securities and Exchange Commission only recognizes accrual-based accounting, a far more accurate indicator of an enterprise's fiscal condition.

States were lulled into complacency because a growing economy propelled increases in stock prices for many years, enhancing the coverage of many pension plans, public and private. Pension systems faced a surplus of funding, and they boosted benefits without regard for future market possibilities. Before the Fed's three-part venture into quantitative easing, interest rates were higher, too. Prudent planning cannot assume that interest rates will rise to prior levels or that stocks will resume their prior course—state budget projections need to reflect this reality. States must devise ways to reduce their debt so as not to burden their taxpayers, present and future.

Even when financial markets perform relatively well, they do not regularly create a return as high as estimates that state pension plans use (usually 8 percent). The past few years have seen large gains in equities, which have helped the balances of pension funds. But when declines and sluggish growth from the previous years are taken into account, funds do not meet rosy projections. There is no tidy approach to resolving these problems. The states are essentially autonomous, free to pass the burdens of their spending to the young.

In other research, the Pew Center on the States, a nonpartisan research organization based in Washington, estimates that 34 states have funding levels below 80 percent of full coverage.[38] In 2010, Wisconsin was the only state with a fully funded public-pension plan.

In the public sector, gains and losses were smoothed over a longer period, typically five years. The Governmental Accounting Standards

Board, a nonprofit organization that influences how governments report their pension finances, is proposing that public-sector plans do away with smoothing and instead use market valuations of their assets.[39] This would correct one of the transparency problems that have led to public funds' incurring greater near-term deficits than private plans. The disparity, and potential effect on future generations, suggests that states and cities need to be disciplined and held accountable.

Even more problematic are the high discount rates used by public-pension plans. These rates cloud the plans' true costs. When a higher discount rate is used, plans appear to be better funded.

Pension plans are supposed to be safe investments. There is no reason to expect a consistent return of 8 percent on investments that are not risky. Using a discount rate that represents actual returns makes plans' fiscal conditions look worse, but showing an accurate picture of funding levels is something that benefits all stakeholders—public-sector workers, retirees, elected officials, and taxpayers. How can policymakers achieve their goals if they do not have a clear picture of what is going on? In other words, lying with numbers does no favors for anyone.[40]

Although private plans can reduce employee benefits and increase contributions to bring underfunded plans into financial health, some public-sector plans have been prohibited by the courts from doing this. New employees can be charged a higher contribution rate for lower benefits, but not current employees who were hired under more favorable terms. A municipality in bankruptcy, such as Detroit, can restructure its pension obligations—but not all cities want to, or should, go bankrupt.

Instead, states could gradually raise the age at which government workers can retire. In some states, employees can quit at 50 and start collecting benefits, at the same time as they get another job—and start accruing a second set of pension benefits. Alternatively, states could allow workers to retire at the same age but postpone the age at which they begin to collect benefits.

States could convert their defined-benefit pension plans to defined-contribution plans, thereby eliminating the addition to future pension liabilities. As to what we must do to fix the current crisis, either older workers and retirees will have to accept lower payments or tax increases will be necessary. The switch to defined-contribution plans has been the trend in the private sector. Only union-managed multi-employer plans are sticking to their defined-benefit status, and many of these are in poor financial shape.

States could also reduce the power of the public-sector unions. Wisconsin, which has the lowest per-person pension liability, passed a law in 2011 stating that joining a public-sector union would be optional and that the state would not collect dues for unions. The percentage of workers belonging to unions in Wisconsin declined from 14.2 percent in 2010 to 11.7 percent in 2013, according to Labor Department data released in January 2015.[41] This decline was driven by a steep decline in public-sector union membership.

With Uncle Sam strapped for funds, it is extremely unlikely that Washington will bail out insolvent state pensions. William McBride of the nonpartisan Tax Foundation has estimated that in order to fund our federal deficits, the federal government would need to raise tax rates on people earning over $250,000 to 90 percent or more.[41] This would not cover our deficits for long, because it does not account for the shrinkage in GDP that would result, which would lower the revenue. This is clearly impossible and impractical, but it shows just how dire America's financial standing has become.

Alternatively, Washington could make up the revenue by doubling all personal income tax rates, so the top rate would be 80 percent and the bottom rate would be 20 percent. This would raise $493 billion per year, accounting for reduction in hours worked due to higher rates, or $1.2 trillion per year, with no change in behavior. Realistically, raising taxes to this extent would lower GDP by more than 12 percent and wages by 3 percent, and would cost the economy more than 3 million jobs.

Another option would be a value-added tax of 10 percent, which could bring in between $500 billion and $1 trillion a year. But this would be vastly unpopular.

These high tax rates are unimaginable and un-American. Something else must be done to bring the financing of Medicare, Social Security, and other federal programs under better control. It is not practically possible to increase taxes enough to get rid of the federal debt. The only solutions are to cut spending or increase economic growth. So far, we've had no success with either of these options.

Take entitlement reforms. Older Americans are too attached to their entitlement programs to cut them, even though keeping the status quo means that young people will pay the price. No president, Republican or Democrat, has succeeded in trimming entitlements. No Congress has passed laws making significant adjustments to the programs. President George W. Bush started exploring Social Security reform in his first term. But it was not until 2004, after winning reelection, that he actively pushed to allow individuals to put a portion of their Social Security contributions into private accounts and then pass the accounts on to their heirs at death. Unfortunately, as with most attempts to take on "the third rail of American politics," his efforts failed. While his proposals were far from perfect, opponents demonized them before the county had a chance to have a constructive public debate, and so we fell deeper into fiscal disarray. Similarly, some individuals and think tanks have suggested solutions to Medicare's fiscal woes, but Americans have yet to support enough politicians who want to put any of these ideas into practice.

One way to inject competition into Medicare is premium support, an idea dating back to the 1997 National Bipartisan Commission on the Future of Medicare, chaired by two retired members of Congress, Representative Bill Thomas (R., Calif.) and Senator John Breaux (D., La.). Thomas and Breaux have retired from Congress, but the Medicare Commission's premium-support idea appears in the House 2013 budget. Modeled after the Federal Employee Benefits Program, it would allow Americans 55 and younger, beginning in 2023, to choose from a variety of government-approved competing comprehensive health-insurance plans, at different prices with different levels of service. Current Medicare recipients would not be affected. Options could include high-deductible plans carrying lower premiums combined with health savings accounts, or more traditional managed-care or fee-for-service plans. Traditional Medicare would continue to be one option. This would lower health-care costs because when people are aware of prices, they spend less. Now the only ones who usually see the prices are insurance companies and the government, who have put themselves in the position of telling people what health care they should have. But the incentives of third-party payers and patients are very different.

America is being driven towards bankruptcy. The federal debt is exploding thanks to historical deficits year after year. The unfunded liabilities of runaway entitlement programs, mainly Social Security and

Medicare, make America's fiscal outlook even more frightening. On top of the federal debt and unfunded liabilities, states have their own fiscal problems. Most state debt is the result of unfunded promises as well.

While the situation is dire, there is hope for reform. The American public has a newfound concern about mounting federal debt—nearly 8 in 10 Americans agree that the national debt should be among Washington's top three priorities—and some members of Congress are starting to respond to public pressure.[42] While righting the course of our fiscal ship will not be easy, delaying action will only make matters worse.

It is the job of those elected politicians at the state and federal levels who said they would tackle the deficit to offer alternatives for debate and discussion, rather than pushing the problem down the road, on the backs of younger Americans. Young people did not incur these debts, and forcing them to face consequences they do not deserve is neither fair nor good for future economic growth.

———— • ————

CHAPTER 2

PAYING FOR PARENTS' HEALTH CARE

I n 2010 Washington passed the Patient Protection and Affordable Care Act, which raised the cost of health insurance for the young and required them to subsidize older Americans. It also increased the cost of hiring, contributing to the slowdown in employment growth that is throwing major roadblocks in the way of young people's careers.

The Affordable Care Act is a sweeping overhaul of America's health-care system that requires nearly everyone to sign up for health insurance and also tells them what kind of insurance they must buy. The law has helped some uninsured people obtain coverage. But millions of Americans have also seen their health-insurance plans canceled, because the plans did not meet the requirements of the ACA, or their plans have become more costly to pay for the roster of newly added benefits. It has enmeshed many in a bureaucratic nightmare.

Tommy Groves, a young professional working at a small firm in Washington, D.C., was one of the nearly 5 million Americans to receive a termination-of-coverage letter in October 2013 from his health-insurance provider, because his previous plan did not comply with the ACA's requirements. While about half the states offered to extend cancelled plans for another year, later increased to two years, the District of Columbia required its residents to get new insurance.

Tommy's employer gives him a set amount each month to cover his health-care premium. Extra money is directed to a health savings account, whose tax-free funds he can use to cover future medical expenses. Because of this system, common to many small businesses, Tommy had no choice but to grudgingly visit D.C. Health Link and attempt to sign up for an insurance plan on the ACA exchange. He did not get very far. Besides the obvious, embarrassing computer difficulties that became infamous on the state and federal exchanges, massive technological problems with "back-end functionality" also plagued the site. D.C. Health Link was unable to verify Tommy's identity, and after hours of back-and-forth on the phone with an ACA help center, he was told to send in a paper application.

In December, Tommy did just that. He still had not heard back at the beginning of January 2014, the date by which he was supposed to be signed up. This deadline was later extended to March 31, 2014. After many phone calls and countless hours on hold over a period of weeks, and despite multiple assurances to the contrary, Tommy was informed at the beginning of February that his paper application had been lost. Finally, in March, close to the March 31 deadline for purchasing health insurance, he was directed to a place where he could sign up in person.

This attempt, too, did not succeed, as the "navigators" there had been instructed not to accept paper applications any longer. Finally, after hours more on the phone with D.C. Health Link over an additional series of weeks, the online system was able to verify his identity, and he met the deadline for purchasing health insurance to begin March 1, although D.C. Health Link refused to let him backdate the coverage to January 1.

Aside from the problem of a government agency's losing sensitive health and identity information, Tommy faced another difficulty. In January, while he was still not enrolled in the exchange, he needed a minor medical procedure. He thought it would be only fair that this expense should be deducted from his new plan's deductible, especially because his health-insurance provider would remain the same under the new plan. This led to another bureaucratic nightmare in which he had to fight both D.C. Health Link and his health-insurance provider. D.C. Health Link tried to pass off the blame to his health-insurance provider, when those at D.C. Health Link were clearly at fault—it was the government that had failed to create a functioning site and that had lost his application, not the private insurance company.

"I don't want everyone who is thrown off their employer's health insurance to go through what I did," Tommy told us. "It was miserable and a complete waste of my time. Nobody listens to you. Nobody takes responsibility. The only advice I tell people who are going to be stuck dealing with the health-care exchanges is, 'Get ready for the bureaucracy.' "

Tommy's premium for his "silver plan" went up to $225 a month from his $175 pre-ACA rate. Both plans cover the health-care services he wants, but his new plan includes services that he does not need, such as maternity care, pediatric dental care, mental-health coverage, and substance-abuse treatment. His deductible increased from $1,400 to $1,500 for in-network coverage, and from $2,800 to $3,000 for out-of-network coverage. Tommy is now paying more for coverage that is less valuable to him, all while he was forced to spend tens of hours on the phone from the end of November to the end of March. And it took until September 2014, five months after he had signed up, for D.C. Health Link to show that he was enrolled.

Young people have no way out of this minefield. They can either buy expensive coverage for services they do not need, or they can pay a fine for refusing to buy insurance under the "individual mandate." No matter which way young people turn, the ACA will take a toll on their pocketbooks.

Since insurance companies are not allowed to charge older people more than three times as much as younger people (a provision known as "modified community rating"), the law artificially holds down the premiums of older people and raises the price for the young. In order to pay for the health-care costs of older people, insurance companies had no choice but to pass those costs on to the young in the form of higher premiums. This is a major factor behind the low number of young people who have signed up for insurance under the ACA.

Before the law, the typical cost of insuring an 18-year-old was one-fifth that of a 64-year-old.[1] Because older people are at a much greater risk of serious health problems than people just out of high school, it makes sense that insurance companies would charge the 64-year-old more. But income typically rises with age, so the 64-year-old in most cases would be better able to afford the higher premiums.

Young people, therefore, not only face higher premiums, but they also have a harder time paying for them. This more than negates the benefits to young people of being able to remain on their parents' insurance plans until they are 26.

In 2013, the White House set a goal that 40 percent of total enrollment in the ACA exchanges should consist of young people between the ages of 18 and 34.[2] President Obama reached out to young people during the ACA open-enrollment period, appearing with youth-friendly comedian Zach Galifianakis on his parody Internet talk show *Between Two Ferns* to promote the law. Joanna Coles, the editor in chief of *Cosmopolitan* magazine, was invited to have lunch at the White House after she publicly declared that she would use her magazine to promote the ACA.

Some organizations have put out troubling advertisements for the ACA that seem to convey that young people care only about partying and sex. The Colorado Consumer Health Initiative and ProgressNow Colorado Education, for instance, released ads for the ACA targeted at young people.[3] One showed a group of college-age men doing a keg stand; the text accompanying the image encouraged young men to get "brosurance." A second ad showed a young woman holding her birth control pills while standing next to an attractive man; they were identified beneath their photo as "Susie & Nate, Hot to Trot." The text on this ad was far more offensive than "brosurance." It read: "OMG, he's hot! Let's hope he's as easy to get as this birth control. My health insurance covers the pill, which means all I have to worry about is getting him between the covers. I got insurance. Now you can too. Thanks, Obamacare!"

Excluding free press by friendly reporters and celebrities, Washington has spent more than $700 million on a public-relations campaign dedicated to selling the ACA to young people.[4] One social-media ad featured a young man wearing hipster glasses and plaid, zip-front onesie pajamas. He's half-smiling and cradling a mug of hot chocolate in his hands. The caption read: "Wear pajamas. Drink hot chocolate. **Talk about getting health insurance. #GetTalking**." (Bold in original.) At times it seemed as if Washington was making a bigger push to sell the law among young people than among its target beneficiaries. By the end of open enrollment in March 2014, 28 percent of enrollees were within the target age range of 18 to 34, even though this age group makes up around 40 percent of the uninsured population.[5] Why should the government spend taxpayer dollars to convince people to purchase a product they are required to buy anyway?

Washington is targeting young people because the costs of their health insurance are high and the benefits they receive are low. They are generally healthy. People under 30 spend on average $600 a year on medical costs ($388 on medical services, $149 on drugs, and $62 on medical supplies).[6] Yet with a silver plan, the average premium for a 27-year-old is $2,680, with an average deductible of $1,842. Premium subsidies would reduce the average premium to $671, but even so, a typical 27-year-old would have to spend $2,513 before getting any benefits.[7] No rational person would want to buy such a product, which is why the government has to spend valuable taxpayer dollars to convince people to sign up. It would be more financially advantageous for young people to pay the fine and skip the coverage.

If only those who most need insurance, such as the elderly, actually buy it, then premiums rise for everyone. This price increase causes more young, healthy people, often called "young invincibles," to drop health-insurance coverage. Only the sickest people will remain, costing the insurance companies even more per enrollee. As this happens, premiums will go even higher, leading to a vicious cycle known as a "death spiral."

This problem can be mitigated if premiums are low enough to encourage healthy people to buy insurance. But, under the ACA, premiums for young people are anything but low. In 2014, 27-year-old males saw their premiums rise an average of 91 percent because of the law. In contrast, premiums for the average 64-year-old rose only 32 percent.[8]

When the ACA's controversial risk corridors and reinsurance bands expire in 2017, premium rates are likely to spike even higher. This will drive even more young, healthy people out of the exchanges. In 2018, if federal subsidies for health insurance exceed half a percent of GDP, premium-subsidy payouts will be cut.[9] Washington's failure to make insurance more attractive to young people today means that the cost of even basic coverage will probably increase sharply in a few years. Insurance coverage at these steep rates will make sense only for those who expect to have high medical costs or risks.

While 91 percent is a major increase, premiums for young people have the potential to rise even more. After all, the law is only in its second year. As more of the law's mandates go into effect in subsequent years, premiums could rise further. A survey of 17 major insurance companies estimated that the new law would lead to a 180 percent premium increase for young, healthy males.[10]

Jason Church, a retired Army officer who was injured in the line of duty, knows the difficulties young people face due to growing health-care costs, many of which are related to the ACA. Jason is covered by the Defense Department's Tricare, so he is free from the direct effects of the ACA as he recovers from his injury. Regardless, he sees what other young people are going through and cannot help but worry about how they will be affected.

"Are enough healthy, young people signing up for the law to cover the costs of insuring older people?" Jason asked us. "I personally would pay the penalty over paying more for insurance coverage I do not need, especially while the penalty is so low. I am sorry for those who have lost their current plans and are stuck shouldering the costs of ACA."

Washington is loath to admit to young people that the health-care law is designed to force them to shoulder the costs of their parents' health care. But the young, it seems, are not biting, as evidenced by their low enrollment rates. Only 28 percent of enrollees in the first enrollment period were between the ages of 18 and 34, well below President Obama's 40 percent target. [11]

Not only will young people be paying higher premiums under the ACA, but they will also be forced to buy plans that cover health services they do not want or need. The ACA mandates that all plans available in the individual market offer an array of "essential health benefits," which, in addition to contraceptive coverage, include maternity and newborn care, mental-health coverage, rehabilitative services, and pediatric care.[12] The average 27-year-old is highly unlikely to require all of these benefits, yet the ACA requires people this age to pay for them nonetheless. Such mandates, though well-intentioned, drive up costs for young people, most of whom only need services such as periodic medical visits and catastrophic care in the unlikely case of a major accident.

Some 35-year-olds might be happy to have their insurance plan cover maternity care, but many twentysomethings—as well as people who have decided not to have children or who are beyond childbearing age—are unlikely to feel the same enthusiasm. It is unfair to ask young people and these other groups to subsidize the maternity care of middle-aged people, especially considering that middle-aged Americans saw the smallest premium increases from the law. Additionally, young singles typically have a lower household income than that of couples who have decided to have children.

Out of households in the top 5 percent of incomes, more than 80 percent are married-couple families. Only 4 percent are males living alone, and another 4 percent are females living alone. On the low end of the income scale, 17 percent of those in the lowest 20 percent of incomes are married-couple families, whereas 57 percent are either males or females living alone.[13]

By requiring all health-insurance plans to cover these benefits that Washington deems "essential," the ACA also reduces competition in the insurance market, which has the dual effect of raising prices and reducing quality. Never mind that it is unlikely that unelected bureaucrats working for the Department of Health and Human Services will know what is best for individuals. The point of private insurance is for people to choose the plan that works best for them, not for other people to tell them what they can and cannot buy.

In a competitive market, health plans that offer maternity care and other specific benefits will endeavor to do so for a low cost relative to value; otherwise, customers will simply purchase plans that do not include those services and pay for those expenses out of pocket. But if everyone is mandated to buy coverage for maternity care, then insurance companies have less incentive to keep expenditures on maternity care down, and costs will rise for enrollees.[14]

Purchasing insurance through the ACA is more like buying electricity from your local electricity company than buying insurance. With electricity, as with other utilities, you have a set service at a set rate and the company's profits are determined by the government. With life insurance, auto insurance, and home insurance, a variety of products are available and companies compete to sell them. With the ACA, it is the government that determines the products that are on offer. This is not true insurance.

An estimated 4 million people, many of whom are young, will pay the fine for failing to purchase approved health insurance in 2016.[15] In 2014, the individual-mandate penalty was $95 per year (rising to $695 in 2016), or 1 percent of income if that amount is higher;[16] the average monthly premium for the lowest-level "bronze plan" for a 27-year-old was $226.[17] This means that young people with average annual health-care costs of

$600 will pay more than $2,700 per year just for insurance premiums.[18] So overpriced is insurance under the ACA that many would rather pay a fine and receive no coverage than buy the insurance.

The ACA creates a disincentive to purchasing insurance—one of the many perverse incentives in the law. Michael Lopato, a recent college graduate who is working as a computer programmer while pursuing a graduate degree, told us why he would not buy coverage if it were not offered through his work. "If people are guaranteed the ability to buy health insurance, even with a preexisting condition, then what incentive would a healthy 25-year-old have to pay thousands of dollars per year for health insurance?" he asked. "Even with a penalty in the hundreds of dollars, it would seem to me that a young man would be better off avoiding purchasing health insurance until he gets some sort of condition that would make purchasing the insurance economically beneficial. Under the previous system, such a person would have an incentive to buy insurance at a younger age, in order to be able to secure a policy when he is afflicted with some sort of condition in the future. The regulation on companies to sell insurance to those with preexisting conditions eliminates this incentive in its entirety." As the ACA enrollment numbers show, Michael is not the only young person thinking this way.

The law's ill effects are not limited, however, to the purchase of expensive health care. Several unintended consequences of the ACA also make it more difficult for young people to find jobs. The employer mandate, for instance, requires employers with 50 or more full-time-equivalent workers (defined as workers who spend 30 or more hours per week on the job) to provide health insurance to their full-time employees or face a fine. Given the soaring cost of health insurance, many employers opt to pay the fine, or else they cut workers' hours to bring them below the full-time threshold. With taxes, the fine is effectively $3,000 per employee. In addition to salary costs, hiring a 50th full-time worker would cost an employer $60,000 (the first 30 workers are exempted from the fine).[19] This constitutes a major deterrent to expansion, costing the economy jobs.

Some of the people who are the hardest hit by the employer mandate and penalty are those who work in the leisure and hospitality fields, such as restaurant workers. These industries have traditionally offered the greatest opportunities to young, entry-level workers, but many do not offer health insurance to all their employees, who are often part-time, temporary workers with flexible schedules.

Small businesses are also disproportionately affected by the employer mandate. President Obama implicitly admitted this by delaying the employer mandate two additional years for firms with fewer than 100 employees: They are now exempt from the fine until January 2016. Small businesses that cannot afford to pay the fines will either refrain from hiring new entry-level workers or hire them only on a part-time basis, reducing the number of full-time jobs available.

The threat of the employer mandate is already having repercussions on the availability of jobs. Twenty-seven percent of franchise businesses, which frequently employ entry-level workers, have replaced full-time workers with part-time workers.[20] This trend will only get worse; 64 percent of franchise managers expect that the ACA will have a negative effect on their business.[21] Business requires planning ahead, and when such a large percentage of American business owners are apprehensive about what the ACA will bring, it does not bode well for robust economic expansion.

Before the recession, in December 2007, 17 percent of workers were part time and only 4.5 million people were working part time for economic reasons—meaning that they wanted but could not find full-time work. Now there are 26.5 million part-time workers in America, 18 percent of total employment. Of these, 6.8 million are working in part-time jobs for economic reasons.[22] Though the ACA is not solely responsible for these increases, it deserves some blame. As the labor-market repercussions of the Affordable Care Act begin to take effect in full force, the number of part-time workers will probably rise.

Unemployment among young people is already at the unacceptable level of over 13 percent. Labor-force participation among young people is also low, around 55 percent compared with 63 percent for the broader population, levels comparable to what they were in 1978.[23] Young people have been the biggest losers in the economic recovery. Do we really need the ACA hampering their employment prospects even more?

A 2014 report by the center-left Urban Institute found that eliminating the employer mandate would have little effect on total health-care coverage, increasing the number of uninsured by only 0.07 percentage points. After all, only 4 percent of firms with 50 or more workers do not already offer health insurance as a benefit, with most of those firms having fewer than 100 full-time-equivalent employees.[24] As firms expand and seek new hires, most will start offering health insurance as a benefit in order to retain their skilled employees and entice new ones. But the ACA does not allow firms to make that transition when it makes the most economic sense to them. It instead opts for a one-size-fits-all solution that results in massive disincentives to hiring and penalizes small businesses that are struggling to expand.

Labor unions are taking notice of these disincentives to hiring. In 2013, the leaders of three major unions, including the Teamsters, sent a letter to Democratic leaders in Washington protesting several provisions of the ACA, including the employer mandate:

> [T]he law creates an incentive for employers to keep employees' work hours below 30 hours a week. Numerous employers have begun to cut workers' hours to avoid this obligation, and many of them are doing so openly. The impact is two-fold: Fewer hours means less pay while also losing our current health benefits.... On behalf of the millions of working men and women we represent and the families they support, we can no longer stand silent in the face of elements of the Affordable Care Act that will destroy the very health and well-being of our members along with millions of other hardworking Americans.[25]

It is encouraging to see those who are traditionally enthusiastic supporters of expanded government benefits, such as labor unions, waking up to the reality that the employer mandate, among other provisions, will be terrible news for the labor market. With the Congressional Budget Office estimating that 30 million people will remain without insurance in 2016 even with the provisions of the ACA, the predicted coverage losses from eliminating the employer mandate are miniscule compared with job losses resulting from the massive disincentives to hiring created by the mandate.[26]

The great irony of the employer mandate is that it is not even integral to the functioning of the ACA. The administration has twice bypassed Congress to delay the employer mandate; it will now take full effect in 2016, although the text of the bill stated that it should take effect in 2014.

If this were a central aspect of his signature piece of legislation, the president would not have unilaterally delayed it multiple times.

The ACA's 2.3 percent medical-device tax and its billions in yearly pharmaceutical fees are also driving up the cost of insurance. As with the other taxes, these costs are passed on to employers and individuals in the form of higher premiums. The young, who use far fewer medical devices and medications, are stuck with the tax bill for products they do not often need.

Another costly provision of the ACA has not yet taken effect, but when it does, it will surely have an adverse effect on employees. The "Cadillac tax," set to begin in 2018, is a 40 percent excise tax on insurance plans that cost more than $10,200 per year for individuals or $27,500 for families. Such expensive plans are common in the market for employer-provided health insurance, so the costs of a 40 percent excise tax are almost certain to be passed on to employees in the form of reduced wages and other benefits. A survey of private employer-sponsored health plans revealed that most employers cite the Cadillac tax as their number-one complaint when it comes to providing health insurance.[27]

The Cadillac tax was intended to hold down the growth of expenditures of health insurance by penalizing insurance plans over a certain, seemingly arbitrary, premium threshold. But the ACA does little to address the underlying causes of the growth in health-care costs, such as preferred tax treatment for employer-provided health insurance or excessive medical-malpractice insurance costs. The Cadillac tax will only serve as a greater strain on American workers already struggling in the prolonged economic recovery. The result will be lower take-home wages, which will especially affect young people who are starting their careers. Instead of helping young people move up the economic ladder, the ACA keeps them stuck on the first rung or flat on the ground.

The Congressional Budget Office projects that the ACA will reduce employment in the United States by the equivalent of 2 million full-time workers by 2017 and 2.5 million by 2024, almost entirely because workers are choosing to work less.[28] This comes on the heels of a worrying decline in the labor-force participation rate from above 66 percent in the years before the recession to below 63 percent in 2014.[29]

In May 2010, Representative Nancy Pelosi (D., Calif.) said, "We see [the ACA] as an entrepreneurial bill, a bill that says to someone, if you want to be creative and be a musician or whatever, you can leave your work, focus on your talent, your skill, your passion, your aspirations, because you will have health care."

But the *Merriam-Webster Dictionary* has a slightly different definition of "entrepreneur" than does the former speaker of the House.[30] It defines "entrepreneur" as "one who organizes, manages, and assumes the risks of a business or enterprise." Being an entrepreneur takes more than pursuing passion projects. Young people need to be gaining work experience, not sitting around in plaid onesie pajamas while sipping hot chocolate. Not only is robust labor-force participation necessary to sustain economic growth, as we see in the counterexample of Western Europe's stagnant economies, but unfunded programs such as Social Security need a supply of young workers paying taxes to keep them from going into default, as was described in Chapter 1.

For some young people, working less is a setback that leads to long-term negative economic consequences. Having a full-time job is a crucial signal to employers that prospective employees can create value for an organization and are dedicated workers. Additionally, missing out on the hard and soft skills learned from work, those that school cannot teach, leads to diminished human capital, fewer future opportunities, and reduced earnings.

In his latest book, *Side Effects: The Economic Consequences of the Health Reform*, University of Chicago economist Casey Mulligan illuminates part of the reason that individuals choose to work fewer hours, or supply less labor, under the ACA. One of the law's little-known provisions disallows full-time employees and their families from receiving federal subsidies on the government exchanges if their employers offer what is deemed affordable coverage. In order to be eligible for federal subsidies, employees must work part time. According to Mulligan, this is equivalent to a tax on full-time work, because moving from part-time to full-time work will entail the loss of the federal health-insurance subsidy. As with everything else in economics, if you want to get less of something, tax it. If improved standards of living are the goal, it is neither wise policy nor sound economics to place additional taxes on productive work.

When working more hours results in the loss of government aid such as insurance subsidies, it is economically equivalent to a tax on labor. Under the ACA, therefore, effective tax rates on an additional hour of labor can exceed 100 percent. People to whom this effective tax applies will take home more money by working fewer hours, which also means they would lose money by working more—bad news for America's labor supply and economy.

Young people are twice as likely as the overall population to be subject to this perverse tax. According to Mulligan's analysis, 9.7 percent of workers younger than 25 could face a penalty for working full time, versus 4.7 percent for the population as a whole. Among workers ages 55 to 64, only 2.7 percent are at risk for this penalty.[31]

Young people need to be in the workforce full time, building their human capital by acquiring skills that will make them more valuable to employers. This is how people advance in their careers—by working entry-level jobs to gain experience that they can bring to higher-paying jobs later in life. The ACA encourages them to stay in low-wage jobs, or out of the workforce altogether, by providing strong incentives for part-time work or no work at all, as opposed to full-time employment.

If the ACA remains on the books, it will become another entitlement program similar to Medicare that will drive up the federal deficit over the coming years. Unfortunately, as with other entitlements, the ACA will be paid for by young people when the bill eventually comes due. CBO projects that over the next decade, the ACA will add a net $1.4 trillion to the deficit, since the costs of insurance subsidies and Medicaid expansion far outstrip the revenues raised from new taxes and penalties, as damaging as these are.[32] By 2039, under current law, federal expenditures on major health-care programs, including exchange subsidies, are expected to be 8 percent of GDP, a historically unprecedented amount.[33]

Charles Blahous, a public trustee for Social Security and Medicare, argues that there could be further hidden costs in the ACA that have the potential to worsen an already-dire fiscal picture. He predicts that per-person health-care spending on the uninsured will rise by 39 percent,[34] a prediction backed up by a 2014 Harvard University study.[35] Moreover, many provisions of the ACA designed to raise revenues have not been enforced, such as the employer-mandate penalties.

Retired Army officer Jason Church sees this as a part of a larger problem: Rising government-funded medical expenses are bankrupting America. "Life expectancy keeps increasing, and while that is a good thing, medical expenses are rising with them," he told us. "Money doesn't grow on trees, but our elected officials are pretending it does. The spending on major entitlement programs is set on autopilot, and all it does is keep going. Something has to give. Unfortunately, either interest rates on our debt will rise (eating up an even larger amount of tax dollars), or the programs will have to be flipped on their heads—robbing millennials of the benefits they have been stuck funding for others."

The quality of health care and accessibility are apt to decline as well. The National Health Service in Britain has provided free health care since 1948. Yet a study by the U.K.'s Royal College of General Practitioners estimates that in 2015 there will be more than 50 million occasions when English patients will be unable to get an appointment for at least a week when they need one.[36] Like the United States, the U.K. is experiencing a shortage in general practitioners and specialists. The Association of American Medical Colleges projects that there will be a shortage of more than 130,000 physicians by 2025 in the United States.[37] Both the quality and accessibility of care will decline as this shortage worsens and the United States moves closer to the English model of health care. Despite the best intentions of the lawmakers and staffers who drafted the Affordable Care Act, putting in place more and more levers by which government controls the health-care market is not leading to more-accessible or lower-cost care.

Instead of creating unnecessary market distortions, Washington should strip away the burdensome regulations it has imposed on the health-care market. This would go a long way toward making coverage affordable for young people. Washington should repeal the ACA's "essential health benefits" requirements, so that young Americans would not be forced to buy coverage they do not need. It should also increase competition in the health-insurance market by allowing people to buy insurance across state lines and affording individuals the same tax preferences on health insurance that employers currently receive. Until steps such as these are taken, the war against America's youth will only accelerate, especially in health care.

The pre-ACA status quo in the health-insurance market was not optimal, but Washington has made matters far worse, especially for young Americans. In order to truly help the uninsured, Washington legislators should repeal the ACA and create a tax credit or deduction to allow people to buy any insurance plan that suits them with pre-tax dollars; this would remove one of the main benefits now bestowed unequally on employer-provided coverage. A government takeover of the health-insurance market, with huge repercussions for the labor market and the federal budget deficit, is a terrible way to fix the problem.

While the ACA harms young people such as Tommy who have just entered the job market, other government policies hurt even younger people who are years from entering the workforce. In the next section, we turn to the primary-education system and consider why it is failing America's youth.

PART II

KEEPING YOUNG PEOPLE UNEDUCATED

Not only will millennials be required to pay the deficits incurred by previous generations, but federal and state governments are making it hard for young people to get the high level of education they need to land well-paying jobs. This part of the book discusses the impediments young people face in their education. In primary and secondary education, the subject of Chapter 3, we look at the pattern of older teachers being kept on the job even when they are not qualified to teach. In Chapter 4, we describe the college loans that young people shoulder when they attend college. Those who take out college loans graduate with an average of $27,000 in debt and often few prospects for employment.

Education, the means of acquiring human capital, is one of the most important investments people can make in their future. Oscar Cardoza, a maintenance worker in South Carolina who came from Argentina 20 years ago, told us, "*La educacion es lo solo que va a cambiar la gente.*" ("Only education will be able to change people.") Better-educated individuals command higher wages and a healthier standard of living. Yet at all levels of education, entrenched interests hold back young people who will have to pay high taxes in the future to fund current levels of government spending.

That American primary education is in a state of disarray is not a controversial statement. On the Programme for International Student Assessment (PISA) exam, an international achievement test taken by students all over the world, American students perform in the middle of the pack, far behind South Korea, the Netherlands, and many others. Our high school graduation rate, once the highest in the world, has slipped to 80 percent, and is as low as 50 percent in some urban areas such as Los Angeles. Parents fear for their children's safety in many public schools.

Teachers' unions, one of the most powerful special interest groups in the nation, continually lobby against commonsense education reforms and in favor of rules that keep in place their worst-performing members—all at the expense of students. Bright, young, effective teachers are shortchanged by older, protected ones. All the while, teachers' unions consistently fight educational innovations such as charter schools and voucher programs that have been repeatedly proven to improve educational outcomes, especially for students from low-income families.

Many of the 80 percent of high school students who graduate go on to college. But here, too, Washington makes it more difficult to receive a solid education. Costly programs for student loans, while created with the laudable goal of helping students, have instead sent the costs of a four-year college degree skyrocketing. Students with college loans graduate with a large debt burden that lowers their disposable income and delays significant milestones such as marriage and home ownership.

Students ought to be able to take advantage of attractive alternatives such as community colleges and vocational schools. But here well-meaning high school guidance counselors, fearing the stigma of alternative schooling, insist that students attend a four-year college even if it is not in the individual's best interests. As a result, many young people pay to pursue degrees they will never complete, or they graduate with degrees that will serve them poorly when they seek jobs. Underemployment makes it that much more difficult to pay off a crushing student debt burden.

Although some state and local governments have allowed alternatives such as charter schools, in many instances government fails to help young people who are seeking better education. An under-educated workforce threatens the nation's ability to generate economic growth. By preserving policies that mire our education system in mediocrity, America sacrifices its future. This section explains these policies and describes how we can harness innovation to give the younger generation the education it deserves.

———— ● ————

CHAPTER 3

THE FAILURE OF PRIMARY AND SECONDARY EDUCATION

With young people facing higher bills for taxes, health insurance, and student loans, we would expect states to do everything possible to improve education and raise graduate earnings. But policies favoring old over young are evident throughout the education system, from kindergarten through college. America's top universities remain the envy of the world, but our primary-education system has fallen behind the rest of the developed world's. The Netherlands, South Korea, and Chile—among others—have developed their education systems to make them more competitive on the global scale. Their wisdom is lost on America.

With American's public schools in disarray, promising young teachers such as Kimberly Tett, a 2013 graduate of Augustana College, are choosing to apply their talents at charter schools, which do not offer tenure or require their teachers to join unions as a condition of employment. Kimberly chose to teach literature at an inner-city charter school in Chicago rather than a suburban public school, and she explained her decision to us. "I love the freedom that my charter school gives me when it comes to curriculum," she said. "I can teach literature that I am passionate about, and that passion shows through to my students, and if I'm halfway through the year and the next book I have planned won't work, I have the freedom to make the decision to change it based on what I think will work best for the students and myself. At my charter school, each teacher, whether a rookie or a veteran, has an instructional coach. I am observed by my instructional coach at least once a week, and each observation is followed by a 45-minute meeting. In these meetings, we discuss areas of success, improvement, data analysis, next action steps, etc. Through these meetings and observations, I feel I have grown more as a teacher in just one year than some teachers ever do."

This focus on improvement is having real payoffs for students. A stunning 94 percent of high school seniors at Kimberly's school are accepted into four-year colleges. For Chicago public schools, the college-acceptance rate hovers around 50 percent. Math-proficiency gains are three times higher for students at Kimberly's school than for those in public schools, and ACT scores are also higher. Charter school admittance is determined by a lottery, not by academic record, which strongly suggests that most of these student improvements are a direct result of different approaches to teaching.

In 2009, over the protests of Randi Weingarten, head of the American Federation of Teachers, New York City and the Department of Education tried to close two D-grade public schools in Harlem. The schools had space for 628 and 1,007 students, but enrolled only 288 and 310, respectively; the city planned to replace them with charter schools. Parents were doing everything in their power to avoid living in the neighborhoods within those schools' tracts. Still, Weingarten and her union successfully fought to keep them open. By contrast, Harlem's charter schools that year had 6,000 applicants for only 500 slots.[1]

The main problem with our public-education system is that it favors older, unqualified teachers over the interests of the young. In most fields, if you cannot do your job, you are replaced with someone who can. But not in education. First, measuring teaching ability is not simple, and matching teachers with students is not always easy to do—especially if parents are not allowed to choose their children's schools. Second, unqualified teachers can often stay on because they are protected by unions.

In 2012, American 15-year-olds scored several points below the Organisation for Economic Cooperation and Development average on the PISA examination in mathematics, considered the gold standard for international testing. Their peers in Vietnam, Russia, China, and most of Europe all scored higher than children in America.[2] The country that landed on the moon and that has produced some of the world's greatest innovations is now behind in math and science.

Children in the OECD member nations and in China, Vietnam, and Russia have longer school days and more days in the school calendar than do American children. Plus, when children in other countries are at school, they have fewer hours of sports, assembly, and politically correct programs connected with, for instance, Women's History Month and Earth Day. Young Americans are often not taught difficult subjects, such as advanced literature or history, serious mathematics, hard sciences, or in-demand skills such as computer programming. Schools have dropped useful, career-oriented skills such as wood shop and auto mechanics.

Even if children do not do well in watered-down curricula, they are shuffled along to the next grade. The Board of Education is more interested in pleasing parents than in providing a solid curriculum. In order to graduate, some students have to have a certain number of hours of community service, but they do not have to meet standards in reading or math.

This is part of a pattern of American education that measures inputs rather than outputs. We measure hours of attendance and hours of community service rather than skills acquired. We often give extra credit for effort, but we do not require higher levels of competency in order to earn a high school diploma.

In contrast, many countries around the world focus high school graduation on a final set of exams, whether General Certificates of Secondary Education in the U.K., the baccalaureate in France, or the Abitur in Germany. They do not consider hours of community service or level of effort; what matters is how well young people can demonstrate what they have learned. The result is predictable. Countries that evaluate young people on outputs such as how well they perform on an exam produce students who are more competent than those in countries that measure inputs.

In America, only 80 percent of high school students graduate in four years, a share that declines to 65 percent among African Americans. In many urban areas, barely half of students graduate from high school.[3] Meanwhile, results from the National Assessment of Educational Progress show that only 38 percent of high school seniors are proficient in reading and only 39 percent are proficient in math.[4] In some of the country's major urban areas, the results are even worse. In Chicago, 21 percent of eighth-graders are proficient in reading. In Detroit, it is only 9 percent.[5]

On the PISA exam, 26 percent of American 15-year-olds are designated "low achievers" in math. The OECD average of low achievers is 23 percent. The number is much lower in education powerhouses such as the Netherlands (15 percent), Finland (12 percent), and South Korea (9 percent).[6]

About 32 percent of American students are proficient in math, according to calculations done by a team of education experts. This is below most other developed countries and far short of leaders such as South Korea (58 percent) and Finland (56 percent). In terms of reading, 31 percent of American students are proficient; here we stack up slightly better against our European counterparts. But South Korea, Finland, Japan, and Canada still outperform us by 10 or more percentage points.[7]

Think about this: In some of our major metropolitan areas, fewer than 10 percent of students meet standards of literacy for their age. With so few students armed with basic skills, the consequences for students' future careers and their earnings potential—and for our workforce—are dire. A survey by the Society for Human Resource Management found that 34 percent of employers rated their recently hired high school graduates as "deficiently prepared" for the workforce.[8] It is a local and national crisis, yet few administrators are rushing to change the system.

Despite young Americans' poor performance, one area in which the nation excels is self-esteem. Eighty-four percent of American eighth-graders agreed with the statement "I usually do well in mathematics," with 39 percent of eighth-graders agreeing "a lot." This confidence does not translate into academic performance, however—in Singapore, where only 64 percent of eighth-graders have confidence in their math ability, the least-confident group of students outperforms the most-confident group of American students on international math assessments.[9]

Immediately after World War II, the United States had better high school graduation rates than any other country did.[10] How have we fallen so far?

Many believe that systemic poverty and underfunded schools are the cause of students' poor performance. But in the last 40 years, school funding has exploded. The annual per-student cost of primary and secondary education in America is more than $13,000. After adjusting for inflation, this amounts to an increase of 239 percent over the last half century. America spends more on education per student than any other country in the world, yet average student achievement is only mediocre.[11] Contrary to what many education advocates argue, increased spending by itself has not helped and will not do so in the future.

Nor is inequality of school funding the reason for poor performance. Thanks to federal programs such as Title I, school districts with wildly varying amounts of tax revenue still fund their schools in roughly comparable amounts. More than half of public schools receive Title I funding, serving 21 million students.[12] A Department of Education report found that there is only an 8 percent difference between revenues received per student in the highest-poverty districts versus the richest districts.[13] Yet gaps in student achievement persist, despite the best intentions of federal policymakers.

The tripling of funding to schools has not benefited the young. Powerful teachers' unions have directed this funding into new hires and pay raises for themselves, as student achievement has stagnated. In the 40 years since 1970, the public school workforce has almost doubled to 6.2 million, while student enrollment has gone up by less than 10 percent.[14]

Many of these new hires are not teaching students. In New York City, for example, the local chapter of the United Federation of Teachers in 1995 pushed through a rule that teachers cannot be assigned to non-classroom duties such as patrolling hallways or monitoring lunchrooms. To do this, the school must hire unionized aides—driving up costs with no improvement in student achievement. The rule was relaxed in 2005, but it still limits the number of non-classroom duties teachers can perform, with teachers chosen for the duties in order of reverse seniority.[15]

This problem extends far beyond New York City. Throughout the United States, half of all public school staff members now work in non-teaching roles. Their salaries account for one-fourth of educational expenditures. Support-staff alone makes up 30 percent of school employees. Since 1993, the number of teachers for 1,000 public school students has increased by 5 percentage points. Over that same time, the number of non-teachers per 1,000 students increased 11 percentage points.[16] This trend is not new. From 1950 to 2010, non-teaching positions in public schools increased by 700 percent while the number of students doubled and teaching positions increased by 250 percent.[17]

Some of the increase in funding has also gone to inflating teachers' salaries, with little effect on student outcomes. From 1960 to 2012, teacher salaries rose by approximately $18,000 after adjusting for inflation, an increase of 46 percent. The average teacher is now paid around $57,000.[18] The best teachers are doubtlessly being paid too little, but higher salaries for the worst are a gross waste of taxpayer dollars.

First-class teachers are a school's best investment. If we rank teachers according to quality, replacing a teacher in the bottom 5 percent with a teacher of average quality will generate an extra $250,000 in lifetime earnings for a 28-person classroom (about $9,000 per student). With 3.3 million public school teachers in the nation,[19] replacing the bottom 5 percent (approximately 165,000 teachers) would increase the lifetime income of America's students by $41 billion. Improvements in teacher quality have also been associated with increases in college attendance and reductions in teen birth rates.[20]

In Singapore, Finland, and South Korea, three of the top countries in terms of academic performance, all primary and secondary school teachers come from the top third of their college class. In the United States, only 23 percent of new teachers come from the top third of college students.[21] The future of American education relies on a supply of talented individuals who want to teach. International data show that having teachers with higher cognitive abilities leads to significant increases in students' math and reading scores.[22]

In many cities with abysmal school systems, teacher firings, thanks to powerful teacher's unions, are exceedingly rare. In New York City and Chicago, barely 1 in 1,000 teachers loses his job for poor performance.[23] In Los Angeles, fewer than 2 percent of teachers are denied tenure—and only 0.25 percent of teachers who received tenure were fired over the course of a decade. Meanwhile, graduation rates are barely above 50 percent.[24]

By contrast, between 1 and 2 percent of lawyers and doctors can expect to lose their license to practice over their lifetime.[25] Unions claim that teachers are not being paid enough, which may be true in some cases. But in America's highest-paid professions, a high salary comes at the cost of lower job security and is based on quality of work. Before we raise the pay of teachers, we must first do away with tenure and seniority protections.

In New York City, protections for teachers are so stringent that the worst teachers were sent to "rubber rooms" while their firings went through years of litigation. In these rubber rooms, teachers received full pay and benefits while the school system hired substitutes to teach their classes. The hearings to fire these teachers lasted an average of 502 days and cost $216,588 per teacher. However, fewer than 10 percent of teachers against whom the city brought cases were successfully fired—and many bad teachers do not even make it to the rubber-room stage.[26] Rubber rooms cost the city tens of millions of dollars per year. Were the protections afforded bad teachers not available, that money could have gone toward measures such as improved technology in the classroom, better teachers, or additional after-school programs. These would be far more effective at improving students' lives and educations than are rubber rooms.

All 10 states in the best financial shape in terms of state debt (including unfunded liabilities) per capita are right-to-work states, where employees do not have to be represented by a union as a condition of their employment. In contrast, among the 10 states in the worst financial condition, only Nevada and Wyoming are right-to-work states.[27]

Public-sector unions cannot force government employees to become members but, because all public-sector workers are covered by the same collective-bargaining agreement, employees who opt out still are required to pay agency fees. Agency-fee payers lose some benefits of union membership, such as liability insurance for teachers, but have to pay for *all* union activities except those that are narrowly defined as political. The line between political and nonpolitical spending is often blurred, leading to constitutional questions over collective bargaining's violation of the First Amendment. These issues all date back to the flawed 1977 Supreme Court case, *Abood v. Detroit Board of Education*.

A group of California school teachers is currently seeking to have the Supreme Court reevaluate and overturn *Abood*. In the 1977 case, collective bargaining was upheld, along with forced dues collection, even if members disagreed with the political ideology of the union leadership. *Friedrichs v. California Teachers Association* is now working its way through the courts and offers hope that judges will put an end to the injustice created by taking away choice.

When we spoke with Rebecca Friedrichs, the lead plaintiff in *Friedrichs* and a veteran elementary school teacher, she explained why she needed to lead the lawsuit:

Under California law, teachers must pay "fees" of approximately $650 to $850 per year to the California Teachers Association or the California Federation of Teachers as a condition of employment. We cannot opt out of these fees, which represent the union's one-sided estimate of its collective-bargaining expenses, as opposed to its "overt" political expenses. There is no unbiased oversight to support teachers in the collection of data to discover exactly where our money is directed by union leadership, but many teachers know that the majority of our coerced fees are actually used to push a political agenda with which we do not agree.... In truth, the difference between the union's overt political activities and its collective-bargaining activities is fictitious. Teachers can "opt out" of the "overt" political dues (an additional $350 in my district), but most teachers avoid opting out because doing so leads to a loss of the benefits of membership, which include the right to vote within collective bargaining and essential liability insurance. I have opted out of the overt political portion of my dues; however, I am forced to subsidize the union's efforts to drive up teacher salaries and increase generous pension benefits at a time when California is in a state of economic contraction and cities and localities are going bankrupt. I fundamentally disagree with the union's political position about how public resources should be allocated, yet I am forced to fund the union's position. This trend of unfunded promises that are bankrupting our municipalities has its roots in union domination over the public purse. Union dollars amassed through mandatory dues are used to control elected officials who create laws that are friendly to unions without consideration for the greater good of society. The only way to stop this unfair and destructive trend is to outlaw the collection of coerced union fees."

Rebecca also told us a story about the effect of union protections on students, from when she was first starting out teaching. "My first experience with union abuse was during my year as a student teacher in 1987," she said. "Every day, I watched in horror as a neighboring teacher yelled at and belittled her adorable first-grade students. They were terrified of her. How could they possibly learn in that environment? When I asked my master teacher what could be done about this unjust and danger-ous situation, she told me that because of tenure laws and strong union advocacy, districts had a hard time ridding themselves of abusive and incompetent teachers. That abusive teacher negatively affected hundreds of children for many years until she finally retired."

Reiterating her point that collective bargaining forces her to personally pay for ends she finds immoral, Rebecca said, "I don't know any educators who would feel good about supporting the abuse of children, yet we're all forced to fund the collective-bargaining arrangements that make these horrific situations possible."

In addition to keeping poorly performing teachers in the workforce, tenure laws also discourage younger, better teachers from using their talents in public school systems. Union rules ensure that teacher pay and bonuses are based on seniority and credentials rather than actual performance. Unions also mandate that in times of budgetary strain when layoffs are necessary, teachers must be fired in order of reverse seniority—meaning that the younger teachers must be laid off to preserve the jobs of older ones, regardless of teacher quality.

Since 1990, the two largest teachers' unions, the American Federation of Teachers and the National Education Association, have spent a combined $114 million on campaign contributions, according to the Center for Responsive Politics. Teachers' unions spent $28 million in contributions in the 2014 election cycle alone. AFT and NEA have also spent $60 million on lobbying from 1998 to 2014. The NEA is the fourth-largest donor in American politics since 1989.[28]

"By any reasonable accounting, the nation's two teachers' unions, the NEA and the AFT, are by far the most powerful groups in the American politics of education," argues Terry Moe, author of *Special Interests: Teachers Unions and America's Public Schools*. "No other groups are even in the same ballpark.[29]"

Even teachers are afraid of union power. This is not a new problem. Seeking to shed light on the union rules that were harming her city's young people, Eva Moskowitz, a former Democratic New York City councilwoman and the current CEO of Success Academy, held four days of hearings in 2003 on the mandates. She reached out to several teachers to ask them to testify. Teachers were sympathetic to her goals, but most refused to speak out of fear of retribution from the union. "I'm not that brave" and "I might be blacklisted" were common responses to her requests.[30]

In the face of all this outrage, there are glimmers of hope. In 2014, the Superior Court for the County of Los Angeles, California, struck down the state's teacher-tenure laws on the grounds that they infringed upon civil rights by keeping poor and minority students in failing schools. The case was brought by nine California students, one of whom had not learned to read by the third grade because of ineffective teachers. The court's logic was sound—for poor families who cannot afford to send their children to private schools or move to neighborhoods with better public schools, teacher-tenure laws are a major stumbling block to the education that means a step up the economic ladder.[31]

Despite the political power of teachers' unions, some cities have been successful in rolling back tenure and seniority regulations. Under the guidance of former schools chancellor Michelle Rhee, the school system in Washington, D.C., implemented a pay system based on performance rather than seniority. Under this measure, teachers rated "highly effective" have the opportunity to earn additional bonuses. These bonuses have the double effect of motivating stronger performance and keeping younger, better teachers in the school system.

In order to receive the bonuses, however, teachers have to give up several job-security protections. Teachers' unions largely oppose the bonuses and favor the protections. That is why most cities have not been able to experiment with innovations such as alternative pay scales for teachers, despite studies showing a strong association between alternative pay scales and student achievement. Another factor is cost—in Washington, D.C., the bonuses can add up to $25,000 per teacher. The payoff is probably worth it in terms of higher lifetime earnings for students, but school districts might not be able to find the extra funding.[32] Surely removing union protections for ineffective teachers in order to retain the most effective ones is a smart use of taxpayer money.

The bonuses have continued under Rhee's successor, Kaya Henderson, and preliminary studies have shown that their effect is positive and substantial, especially when teacher evaluations are based on comprehensive assessments rather than strictly on test scores. The merit pay, combined with the threat of dismissal for poor performance, makes bad teachers more likely to voluntarily retire and improves the performance of the teachers who remain.[33] These effects of merit pay are a clear win for students.

One city that has received outside help in implementing merit pay is Newark, New Jersey. The school system received a $100 million donation in 2010 from Facebook founder Mark Zuckerberg, who aimed to improve the school system through the introduction of merit pay. Merit-based bonuses, first paid in 2013, have the potential to improve Newark graduation rates, which currently stand below 70 percent.[34] Last year, nearly 200 teachers in Newark received bonuses totaling $1.3 million.[35]

Education improves when providers are allowed to innovate. Merit pay for teachers is one such innovation. Another approach is to bring education closer to the home, and the home community, the model taken by the Neighborhood Outreach Connection (NOC) in South Carolina's Low Country. The brainchild of Narendra Sharma, a retired World Bank economist from Fiji, NOC is bringing educational services directly to struggling communities. When NOC comes to a community, test scores go up and crime rates go down.

NOC serves 200 elementary school children in six communities. Children get off the bus and go directly to apartments converted into classrooms, where they get a healthy snack and sit down with professional teachers from the school system to do their homework. Many do not have computers at home, and the laptops in the classrooms are their only opportunity to do computer assignments. By purchasing apartments in low-income housing developments and converting them into classrooms, NOC is succeeding in raising the academic performance among some of the poorest students in the state and the country. Because it is located in the community rather than in the school, NOC is there for the kids when they get off the bus. Sharma gets to know the residents, and they know him.

The project gets results. In 2012, NOC summer-school students scored an average of 56.7 percent in reading versus 43.7 percent for non-NOC students, and 51.1 percent in math versus 48.1 percent for non-NOC students. South Carolina is close to the bottom of the 50 states in the National Assessment of Educational Progress tests. "It is frightening that the achievement gap is very significant in Hilton Head, one of the richest municipalities in the state," Sharma told us. "Why don't we educate our children here?"

NOC's after-school and summer programs increase the school year by the equivalent of 28 days for those students who are signed up. The budget for fiscal 2014 was $304,000, about $1,520 per student. Sharma would like to expand the program in a number of ways. He would like to open the classrooms to add middle school children during the week, and middle and high school students on the weekends. The cost of opening on the weekend to serve two dozen students would be $320 per day, or $640 per weekend. That is about $33,000 a year. Expanding opening hours during the week during the academic year would cost another $14,000.

Small efforts make a big difference. NOC leaders work in partnership with the local school district, and the students they serve score better than their peers in reading and math. It might be more cost-efficient for the school district to fund NOC's programs rather than invest in remedial-education programs of its own.

American students suffer not because we spend too little but because we spend unwisely and inhibit, rather than promote, educational innovation. With relatively meager resources, Neighborhood Outreach Connection, a nongovernmental volunteer group, is helping 200 of the poorest students in America. For a fraction of the hundreds of billions of dollars spent on often-disappointing public school education, Sharma and NOC could help many students actually get ahead. American public education does not need more money. Instead, it needs to redirect its current funds to promising programs such as Neighborhood Outreach Connection.

Another promising development, the growth in charter schools, is exemplifying educational innovation in cities and towns across the country, despite strong opposition from entrenched interests. Charter schools receive public funding but are independently operated. With more flexibility, they provide a worthwhile alternative to traditional public schools. In many areas, interest in charter schools is so high that they must conduct a lottery to determine which students will receive admittance. In 2014 in New York City, 70,700 students applied for 21,000 available places in charter schools.[36] Nationwide, over 1 million young people are on a charter school waitlist.[37]

Teachers' unions often fight charter schools by claiming that they are less accountable to students and families because many operate under less burdensome regulations than do traditional public schools. The real reason for their opposition, of course, is that charter school teachers are not unionized. The reality is that charter schools are much more accountable to young people and their parents than are traditional public schools. If parents do not like their children's charter schools, they can send their kids elsewhere. This threat of exit gives charter schools an incentive to raise the quality of the education they offer in order to retain students.

Despite union scaremongering, the verdict is in on charter schools: The public favors them 2 to 1. Among African Americans, who are arguably the biggest beneficiaries of alternative schooling options, the favorability ratio is greater than 3 to 1. Even public school teachers desert the union position on charter schools by a slim margin—38 percent of teachers favor them, and 35 percent are opposed. Overall, many people have yet to make up their minds about whether they support charter schools: Around 40 percent of people neither support nor oppose them.[38]

But what about the actual effects of charter schools on student achievement? Is the success of Kimberly Tett's school usual? Some of the best academic work in this area has been done by Stanford University economics professor Caroline Hoxby; Sonali Muraka, of the New York City Department of Education; and Jenny Kang, of the National Bureau of Economic Research. It is difficult to distinguish between the effects of the charter schools and the effects of the type of students who choose to attend them. If better-educated parents choose charter schools, their children might show higher achievement no matter what school they attend. If higher-achieving students tend to go to charter schools, then looking at test scores will show that charter school students score higher than traditional public school students, but this could be due to student selection rather than to the quality of the school itself.

In order to maneuver around this selection problem, Hoxby and her colleagues conducted an experiment. Since oversubscribed charter schools must conduct lotteries to select students, part of a pool of charter school applicants will attend the charter school, and the other part, the part that does not win the lottery, will attend traditional public school. Everyone in this pool applied to the charter school, so we no longer have to worry about prior differences between applicants and non-applicants. Hoxby and her colleagues simply compared the achievement of lottery winners with lottery losers to measure the effect of the charter school. This type of study is the gold standard for economic literature.

Hoxby and her colleagues conducted a study designed in this way on New York City's school system, where 94 percent of students who apply to charter schools go through lotteries. The authors found that a student who attended a charter school would close 86 percent of the

"Scarsdale–Harlem achievement gap" in math and 66 percent in reading. The gap represents the difference in student achievement, measured by test scores, between one of the wealthiest neighborhoods around New York City (Scarsdale) and one of the poorest (Harlem). By the end of eighth grade, students who attended a charter school could expect to score 30 points higher on a standardized math test than their peers who missed out on the lottery, substantially narrowing the gap between schools in wealthy and poor neighborhoods.[39]

Charter schools in New York City have a statistically significant positive effect on achievement among students regardless of gender or ethnicity. Additionally, the study shows that student achievement is cumulative: The more time students spend in charter school, the more of the achievement gap they will close.[40] Charter schools are doing more with less money; a 2014 report found that, on average, charter schools receive 28 percent less funding per student than do traditional public schools.[41]

Even so, the study probably underestimates the beneficial effect of charter schools on student achievement. With increasing competition from charter schools, traditional public schools have greater incentives to improve quality in order to retain students. Moreover, charter schools will learn from one another over time about the most effective methods of teaching and management. For instance, Hoxby's New York City study has already found an association between a longer school year and better results from charter schools.[42]

In *Please Stop Helping Us*, author and columnist Jason L. Riley gives us another real-world example of the benefits of charter schools. Success Academy Harlem I, a charter school, shares a building with P.S. 149, a traditional public school. Despite the same location and same socio-economic composition of the two student bodies, the achievement gap between the schools is substantial. At Harlem I, 86 percent of students are proficient in reading and 94 percent are proficient in math. At P.S. 149, only 29 percent of students are proficient in reading and only 34 percent are proficient in math.[43]

The success at Academy Harlem I does not stand alone. Success Academy Bronx 2 had the second-highest math proficiency in New York State, even though the school is in the nation's poorest congressional district. More than 80 percent of Success Academy students live in families with incomes below the poverty line, but students all across the Success Academy network are excelling. If all 32 schools in the Success Academy network were a single, large school, it would rank seventh out of the 3,560 New York State schools in math. Overall, 94 percent of Success Academy students are proficient in math and 64 percent are proficient in English-language arts. The averages for New York City are 35 percent and 29 percent, respectively.[44]

Despite the results of Success Academy, New York City's mayor, Bill de Blasio, tried to limit the program by refusing to grant co-location approvals. Co-located schools share resources such as libraries, gyms, and cafeterias, but they operate as separate entities. Because of New York City's high real estate prices, co-location is not rare; it helps the school district save money and more efficiently use its resources. Over 60 percent of New York City schools are co-located, and there is no discernable effect on public students' academic achievement from co-location.[45] Still, teachers' unions, which were major backers of de Blasio's mayoral campaign, sought to limit the spread of charters by challenging previously approved co-locations. It was not until New York State's governor, Andrew Cuomo, put his support behind Eva Moskowitz and Success Academy that Mayor de Blasio finally backed down and helped broker an agreement.

The requirement that students attend a specific school reduces competition and discriminates against students whose parents cannot afford to live in districts with good schools. Merging districts gives parents a choice of school and highlights the most and least popular schools.

In addition to inner-city charter schools and the other opportunities for educational improvement previously discussed, school-choice programs around the nation and the world continue to improve educational quality. Louisiana has one of the country's most impressive school-choice programs. The Louisiana Scholarship Program allows low-income students from failing public schools to transfer to better public schools or charter schools, or even receive vouchers for private schools. Louisiana's alternative schooling options have been so successful that in 2014 the city of New Orleans closed its last traditional public schools in favor of charter schools and private schools. The change has elevated the city's graduation rate from 54 percent in 2004 to 73 percent today.[46]

In 2014, the Louisiana state legislature passed several expansions of the state's school-choice program. All of these bills passed with bipartisan support, in a sign that school choice is gaining recognition as an effective education policy. Eighty-six percent of Louisiana's scholarship students are African American, demonstrating that the benefits of school choice accrue to traditionally disadvantaged groups.[47] Ninety-two percent of scholarship students' parents report satisfaction with the program.[48]

Washington appears to have a different set of priorities, centered on political correctness rather than student welfare. In 2013, the Department of Justice sued Louisiana to block school vouchers from taking effect in the state, on the basis that the vouchers would upset the racial balance of certain schools and thus interfere with federal desegregation orders—despite the fact that the overwhelming majority of voucher beneficiaries are nonwhite. At one school, the loss of only five white students to a voucher school was enough, in the Justice Department's eyes, to warrant a lawsuit.[49] Desegregation expert Christine Rossell looked at Louisiana's voucher program and found that in most districts, voucher programs actually reduced racial imbalance.[50] The DOJ has since withdrawn its suit, but the fact that it was filed at all on such spurious grounds underscores the extreme hostility of the federal government to state initiatives to improve education.

Perhaps no state provides as much choice to students and parents as Arizona. The state now allows children with special needs and those from low-quality public schools to opt for an education savings account (ESA). The state puts 90 percent of per-student public school funding into each child's ESA, which the family can use for an array of education-related expenses, such as private school tuition, textbooks, tutors, online classes, or even savings for college tuition.

ESAs began in Arizona in 2011 and were expanded in 2013, but preliminary results indicate that parents are highly satisfied with the program. A poll by the Friedman Foundation for Educational Choice found that 71 percent of ESA users were "very satisfied" with the program, compared with only 21 percent who were "very satisfied" with the student's previous public school.[51] While public schools still languish in many places, innovative policies such as Arizona's are improving thousands of young lives.

Other countries have gone further with their school-choice programs. The United States is the only developed nation in which government schools have a near-monopoly on primary education, with 1 in 10 students attending private school. Most other countries have a greater mix of public and private schools; in OECD nations, on average, 15 percent of students attend private school. In countries with robust school-choice programs, the number is even higher—52 percent in Chile and 65 percent in the Netherlands. Most private schools in these countries receive at least some funding from the government, the opposite of the situation in the United States.[52]

In an analysis of school systems around the world, those that had features of a competitive market performed much better than school systems operating under a government monopoly. Market features include entry and exit options for students, different prices, and a variety of products. In addition, the smaller the regulatory burden on schools, the stronger educational outcomes tend to be.[53]

In Colombia, a 1990s-era school-voucher program has been associated with stronger student achievement as well as lower rates of child labor and teenage marriage. Voucher recipients were also 10 percent more likely to finish the eighth grade and could expect to earn higher wages over their lifetime. The Chilean voucher program, designed in consultation with the late Nobel Prize–winning economist Milton Friedman, improved educational outcomes in communities as a whole and not just in private schools.[54] This suggests that educational choice improves outcomes across the board through the creation of more competitive markets.

One study found that an increase in the share of students attending private schools is associated with an increase in test scores, even in public schools. Increases in the share of students attending private schools also reduce spending per pupil in school systems, leading to better outcomes at lower cost.[55] According to Harvard University professor and education policy expert Paul E. Peterson, this implies that increasing the share of U.S. students in charter schools to 50 percent would make the math ability of U.S. students "competitive with the highest-scoring countries in the world."[56]

While test scores are an easy metric, they are hardly the only factor parents consider when choosing children's schools. In an era where many schools have metal detectors and violence is a frequent occurrence, student safety is also a major reason that parents want more choice among schools, according to findings by the Friedman Foundation. In Georgia, which offers public scholarships for students to attend private schools, 38 percent of scholarship students' parents cited "improved student safety" as one of the top three reasons for sending children to private schools.[57] All parents want to know that their children are safe at school, and school-choice programs up the chance that students can focus on learning instead of survival.

Our nation's public schools are failing our students—and the economic consequences are dire. Better-educated students make for a more productive workforce, which not only raises wages but also improves our lives through innovation. The next Elon Musk or Marissa Mayer is probably out there right now, but this gifted individual might be trapped in a failing public school and unable to develop his or her human capital or share his or her talents with the world. Rather than encouraging young minds to flourish, teachers' unions and opponents of educational choice choose to protect their own entrenched interests at the expense of students, to the detriment of our society.

But perhaps more than in any other area, we have cause for hope when it comes to our nation's primary education system. Cities such as New York, New Orleans, and Washington, D.C., are already seeing the benefits of their school-choice programs. Every dollar spent on the D.C. Opportunity Scholarship Program was found to yield $2.62 in benefits from higher graduation rates and increased lifetime earnings—a much better investment than most government programs.[58]

Though America's primary school system may be struggling, our higher education system is still the envy of the world. But government policies hurt the young by increasing tuition costs and saddling young people with debt. Education is cumulative, and a better primary education system should go hand in hand with more efficient universities. In the next chapter we will examine how our higher education system fails students, and how to improve it.

CHAPTER 4

———— ● ————

DROWNING IN COLLEGE DEBT

Berea College, in Berea, Kentucky, is a liberal arts "work" college. Founded in 1855, it was the first college in the American South to be coed and racially integrated.[1] It is different from the myriad of other small, liberal arts colleges across the United States in one other respect: It is free.

Students who attend Berea College pay no tuition. They instead agree to work campus jobs to cover their four years of room and board. This program is aided, in part, through a large endowment. In 2013, Berea's endowment was over $1 billion, and its 11.5 percent return on its endowment was ranked 33rd overall out of U.S. colleges and universities—above Ivy League universities such as Cornell, Columbia, and Harvard.[2]

Berea's students are required to work at least 10 hours every week, performing janitorial, maintenance, or student-service tasks. They also staff the college's businesses (such as the Boone Tavern Hotel), work in the local arts-and-crafts industry, and provide teaching assistance to professors.

Berea operates on a tight budget. Julie Laslo, age 24, has taught at Berea for a little over a year and talks of how thrifty the school's administration is. "You have to send in a formal request if you want an extra pencil," she says. "I was once denied such a request."

Berea should be a model for helping underprivileged students attend college and earn degrees. The school only admits students who require financial aid. Unfortunately, it is one of only eight work colleges in the United States.[3] On the bright side, there is plenty of room for growth.

In contrast to Berea graduates, James Findley (not his real name) was $23,000 in debt when he graduated from a private, four-year university. He thought he would land a job right after graduation, but he was not so lucky. Instead, he moved back with his parents and tried to afford the payments on his student loans.

Many young people today find themselves, like James, in a lose-lose situation. They are told that 21st-century jobs require a college education and that if they do not attend college, they will be unemployable. To get to college, they need loans—loans that they can pay off only if they have jobs. And some graduate with the college loans and are still unemployable.

What to do? Go to a four-year college and risk being unemployed with a debt load of $29,400 (the average amount)?[4] Skip the four-year degree and join the workforce in the low-paying retail or hospitality sector? Or go to community college, where the costs are lower, and choose a high-return profession, such as health care or computer programming? The third decision makes the most sense for many high school graduates, but few college guidance counselors recommend it. Most advise young people to go to four-year college, where they end up drowning in debt.

As college tuition continues to grow, debt loads increase, and delinquency and default rates on that debt rise. It is more important than ever that the young come out of college with promising employment prospects. But the job market continues to be poor, with 11 percent of people between 20 and 24 out of work.[5]

While employment prospects for college graduates are admittedly better than those of non-graduates, who face an unemployment rate of 23 percent, graduates' future outlooks are not always positive. Over 8 percent of graduates younger than 25 are unemployed, compared with 3 percent of graduates older than 25. In 2007, before the Great Recession, only 6 percent of recent college graduates (those under 25) were unemployed. In 2000, at the end of the Clinton administration, it was 4 percent.[6]

Unemployment is bad enough, but underemployment comes a close second. Stacy Bell (not her real name), who graduated from a prestigious university with a degree in women's studies, had to settle for a job at Macy's. She is making $9 an hour, but every day she knows that she did not need to go to college to work at Macy's.

The unemployment of college graduates does not even count those who are employed in full-time in jobs that do not require a college education. Even for those who can find a job, the picture is still not rosy. When you add people like Stacy to the number of people who have become so discouraged that they have given up looking, and the people who are working part time even though they want full-time jobs, almost 44 percent of recent college graduates are underemployed, compared with 34 percent in 2001, according to the New York Federal Reserve.[7] Underemployment has long-lasting effects on those just starting out their careers. Working less robs people of the opportunity to gain skills they need to advance their careers. Additionally, full-time job status is a crucial signal to future employers.

With these numbers, why should everyone go to a four-year college? Many young people benefit from attending a university and studying the liberal arts. This is not the majority, however, and we should not build policy around these individuals. The current federal student loan structure effectively does just that. Washington has removed federal insurance for lenders of student loans and made the federal government the primary direct lender of these loans. But that does not mean the loan system has been fundamentally reformed. Standing at more than $1.1 trillion, student loan debt is widespread and requires those in Washington to think beyond ordinary solutions and put everything on the table—including the federal government's $165 billion annual programs of Pell grants, student loans, and tax credits.[8] The situation has become desperate, and, once again, it is the young who are the losers.

For the almost 40 million who carry student loan debt, the average burden is just under $25,000.[9] Fifteen percent default within the first three years,[10] and the 90-day delinquency rate is 11 percent. This is higher than the delinquency rate for residential real estate loans (3 percent), and the credit card delinquency rate (7 percent).[11]

The number of borrowers owing between $50,000 and $75,000 has doubled since 2004, and the number of those owing more than $200,000 has tripled.[12] During that time, overall student loan debt increased by 325 percent, while all other categories of non-housing debt decreased by 5 percent.[13] Perhaps this explains why Wells Fargo found that one-fourth of millennials do not think college was worth the cost.[14]

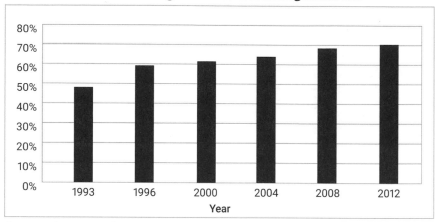

Percent of College Students Graduating with Debt

Year

Source: The Institute for College Access and Success, 2014

Student loan debt is the only household debt that continued to rise during the recession, and young Americans owe more of it.[15] In 2012, 60 percent of borrowers had balances over $10,000, and 30 percent had balances over $25,000. The average balance per borrower was over $27,000. By the end of 2012, over 40 percent of 25-year-olds had student loan debt—debt they cannot shed in bankruptcy despite high delinquency and default rates.[16]

For recent graduates, the burdens are even heavier. For the class of 2012, nearly 70 percent of college graduates needed student loans, and debt at graduation approached $30,000. These recent graduates differ drastically from the class that graduated college in 1993, when less than half of students needed loans before they could walk across the stage to receive their diplomas. In constant dollars, these loans averaged below $10,000—one-third of today's average debt load.

Annie Johnson (not her real name) is a graduate of a small liberal arts college. Even though Annie received a scholarship and attended community college for two years, she is $70,000 in debt. This debt limits her career options and makes living on an entry-level salary difficult.

"It's both absurd and terrifying how the costs of college have shot up," Annie told us. "The way we price education is bloated—meaning we are paying for things that have no value to us. Why is it that college costs keep climbing so much faster than prices in the rest of the economy?"

"My student loan bills are nearly $900 a month," Annie continued. "I see a quality-of-life difference between myself and my friends who do not have student loan debt. I'm at my capacity. Saving is really hard when living expenses are added to my student loan payments. I know this is already setting me back in terms of retirement savings. My future options are limited since, in order to advance my career, I have to go back to school. But to go back to school, I would have to add to my debt."

Annie told us that she hopes to have her student loans paid off by the time she is in her mid-30s, but she thinks that will be difficult to do if she returns to school.

Average Debt for Graduating College Seniors with Loans, Constant Dollars

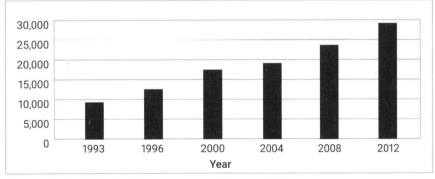

Source: The Institute for College Access and Success, 2014

No one wants to get a loan. Far better to be able to pay for college out of current income, or, even better, have parents pay. But this is no longer possible for most people. College tuition has increased by 1,180 percent since records began in 1978—while food costs have risen only 240 percent over the same period.[17]

Not only does the government's $165 billion annual spending on Pell grants, student loans, and tax credits do little to offset the burden, but it may be contributing to the problem. Rather than fulfilling their original mission of opening the doors of the ivory tower to low-income students, government financial-aid programs have raised the costs of higher education.

William Bennett, secretary of education from 1985 to 1988, coined the "Bennett hypothesis." It goes as follows: "Increases in financial aid in recent years have enabled colleges and universities blithely to raise their tuitions, confident that federal loan subsidies would help cushion the increase." That is why automatically providing student loans through the government (which is how the system has worked since 2010) or offering loans at low interest rates subsidized by the government increases the demand for college education. These low rates allow schools to raise tuition costs exponentially—and they have been doing just that.

The federal loan program is effectively an individually tailored subsidy for each school, because loan awards are based on how much it costs to attend a given college. The more a college raises its tuition, the more loan money the government will make available to students for tuition.

Adding support to the Bennett hypothesis, research by the U.S. Treasury Department found that for every dollar provided in tax-based aid, scholarships fell a dollar.[18] This shifts the tuition burden from students and schools to taxpayers.

Further research on the Bennett hypothesis has shown that not all student loans affect tuition equally.[19] Aid targeted specifically at low-income students, such as Pell grants and subsidized Stafford loans, have less of an effect on rising rates than do universally available loans. The first category of loans allows students who may have not been able to attend college to go; the second type of loan often motivates students to attend more expensive colleges rather than choosing affordable options.

In many cases, students are not getting a better-quality education for their tuition dollars. Much of this funding is going toward administration. From 1976 to 2011, the number of full-time, non-academic professional employees at institutions of higher education grew by 386 percent, while part-time faculty grew by 286 percent. Although many students would benefit from more teaching, tenured and tenure-track professors increased by a meager 23 percent.[20] In addition to the hiring gap, there is also a spending gap: From 1998 to 2008, private research colleges increased spending on instruction by 22 percent but increased spending on institutional support by 36 percent.[21]

College presidents' pay has soared. In 2012, the highest-paid president at a private university was Rensselaer Polytechnic Institute's Shirley Ann Jackson, who received $7.1 million in compensation.[22] Among public universities, the highest-paid president is Ohio State's E. Gordon Gee, who in 2013 received $6.1 million.[23] At the other end of the scale, the president of Purdue University, former Indiana governor Mitch Daniels, receives

$420,000, with an additional $126,000 if he raises student achievement and raises funds.[24]

Tuition dollars also go toward supporting expensive athletic programs. At public four-year colleges in the NCAA, spending per athlete grew by nearly a quarter from 2004 to 2011.[25] Spending increases were even higher for public two-year colleges (35 percent) and private four-year colleges (29 percent). The Knight Commission on Intercollegiate Athletics estimates that public schools in the 11 largest football conferences spent an average of $104,638 per athlete in 2012.[26] From 2006 to 2012, total pay for head football coaches at some Division I schools nearly doubled, to an average of $1,740,646, while professors' pay at those same schools remained relatively flat.[27]

Out of the 45 public university teams in last year's NCAA Basketball Tournament, 41 athletic departments received subsidies that exceeded $420 million in total, for an average of more than $10 million per school.[28] Of this amount, $136 million came from student fees, and an additional $284 million came from nonathletic school funding. When schools subsidize athletics, they divert funds from educational programs to pay for coaching salaries, athletic scholarships, and the maintenance of athletic facilities. Or they raise tuition even higher. Some students want better facilities for their beloved sports teams, but many others wish that instead of building a new basketball arena and athletes-only training rooms, their money was going toward better research facilities, increased financial aid, or lower tuition.

Schools are also spending money on amenities such as rock-climbing walls and golf courses. Massachusetts Institute of Technology has a ball pit to help students relieve stress—some of which might come from the prospect of paying off student debt. Boston University spent $200 million on a fitness center that includes a "lazy river."[29] Colleges justify these expenditures on the grounds of needing to attract the best students. Plenty of students would probably prefer to forgo the rock-climbing walls if it meant lower tuition and a reduced debt burden after graduating.

Universities do not lose by admitting federally subsidized underqualified millennials who do not graduate. The school still receives tuition payments, and if students drop out, other misled freshmen can easily take their places (and their funding) next semester. This incentive to admit government-funded students is evident in how heavily colleges recruit veterans and military members, who receive money for education from the government. Many universities do this, yet only 39 percent of students entering four-year colleges graduate within four years. Within six years of entering college, the number of graduates is still below 60 percent.[30]

Currently, the government has different standards when it comes to for-profit schools such as Corinthian Colleges, which Washington forced to close. These schools, which often provide vocational courses that help students move directly into the job market, have to achieve certain graduation rates or their students cannot receive federal loans. Corinthian relies heavily on revenue from Pell grants and student loan dollars. After the Department of Education withheld this money for three weeks, the chain collapsed.

For-profit colleges offer in-demand technical training and are able to quickly impart knowledge that can help workers keep their trade skills sharp or allow them to move into a new field. However, Washington has decided to wage a war on for-profit colleges rather than preserve their positive aspects. All the while, four-year universities that suffer many of the same ills as for-profit colleges are left alone. This leaves some young people—those who were led to believe that admittance to a four-year school was like winning the lottery—disappointed and discouraged.

What to do? College students would probably make better decisions about their undergraduate education if they knew the worth of their chosen major. Why not publish this information? If Stacy had known that her women's studies major would not land her a job, she might have chosen communications or marketing, fields that lead to broader job opportunities. The prevailing view on college campuses is that the choice of undergraduate major does not matter, but students are learning the hard way that this is not true.

The rationale for using taxpayer funds to pay for higher education is that students do not yet have the means to borrow the sums needed for education, and higher levels of education benefit the public. The late Nobel Prize–winning economist Gary Becker used the term "investing in human capital" to describe this use of funds. But when students cannot get a job upon graduation, either because they were poorly advised and chose the wrong major or they did not apply themselves, something has to change. There are more beneficial ways to spend the $8,000 it can cost per class at a private university.

College should be an investment. If students want to spend their time theorizing about whether Harry Potter is real (the subject of an actual course at Appalachian State University), that is fine. But studying these types of topics might not be an investment in any traditional sense of the word, unless it teaches better writing or thinking skills. It is consumption and should be treated as such, even though college counselors and the media tell millennials that going to a university is an investment sure to pay off in the future. Young adults are borrowing for personal consumption, not for an investment that might benefit them and the economy in years to come.

Brookings Institution scholars Isabel Sawhill and Stephanie Owen found a positive average return on investment from college. But that average, at 10 percent annually, masks a broad distribution. At the low end, it was 6 percent; at the high end, it was 12. Students' choices of major and school have a significant effect on future earnings and loan-repayment potentials.[31] The federal government makes such wasteful investments possible by offering loans and grants to students regardless of their choice of major and college.

Many students do not consider labor-market demand when choosing a major. This could be why 54 percent of recent college graduates are either underemployed or unemployed.[32] Now 115,000 janitors and a quarter of retail salespersons have college degrees.[33] In 1985, 22 percent of majors were in science, technology, engineering, and mathematics (STEM) fields. Today that number is 16 percent.[34] Looking at specific majors, George Mason University economist Alex Tabarrok notes that while 50 percent more students are in college now compared with the percentage of students in 1985, the number of microbiology and computer-science majors has barely increased.[35] The question remains, How can these jobs, or lack of jobs, lead to repaying massive taxpayer-provided debt? The answer: They cannot.

To raise student awareness about costs and benefits of different majors and colleges, President Obama has renewed his calls for significant reforms to financial aid. In his 2014 State of the Union address, he asked government to stop providing money to colleges that are not offering students returns on their investments. The amount of aid and the rates at which students could borrow would be tied to an institution's ranking. The ranking would be based on their tuition costs, scholarships awarded, outstanding loan debts, graduation and transfer rates, and graduates' earnings and career prospects.

Moving forward, Washington needs to do more than rewarding better-performing schools while not punishing poorly performing ones. The president's ideas are far from perfect, but at least they are a start to a much-needed national conversation. Washington could use an opportunity such as this, when both sides of the political spectrum are motivated to work together because they understand the pressing need for reform.

Instead of tying federal funding to the school's performance, we should allow the amount of taxpayer-provided money to vary in accordance with the ability of the student. Currently the same interest rate of 4.66 percent for direct undergraduate loans applies to everyone regardless of future career prospects. Tying the rate paid to past academic performance—in high school, community college, or university—would provide an incentive for students to pick schools that better fit their skills, potential, and ability to pay. The rate should also depend on what major students select, because the choice of major correlates with repayment potential.

Washington does not have a proven track record of correctly setting interest rates. But reforms along these lines would help reduce the amount of student debt, increase the number of graduates, and lead to higher repayment rates. This is because variable rates based on possibility of repayment are important signals to perspective students. Right now, with the uniform interest rate, everyone is receiving the same signal from Washington, even though the right type of education differs drastically from person to person.

To avoid discouraging low-income students, lenders should consider setting lower interest rates for students at community colleges. This would stop people from saying that we are helping STEM majors, who are presumed to be well-off, while hurting poor students who do not currently have the skills to study STEM.

Both Democrats and Republicans have proposed programs to work with companies and community colleges that train students for the workforce. These companies have a better sense of the skills needed today than do Department of Education officials. The American economy continues to move toward jobs that require postsecondary education or training.[36] However, rather than pushing all students to make a commitment to a four-year degree program, counselors should steer some young people—those who might not be ready for such a commitment—toward community colleges.

High school guidance counselors need to reevaluate their bias against advising students to attend vocational school or community college. When time and financial commitments are taken into account, these options can offer better returns for many students. Young people should not make decisions that have long-lasting financial ramifications without considering all available options. Guidance counselors are doing a disservice to students when they encourage them to attend expensive four-year universities. There should be no stigma attached to attending community college or vocational school. As Governor Pat McCrory of North Carolina said at a General Electric Forum in 2014, many lucrative jobs, such as welding, require hard technical skills that universities fail to teach.

Community colleges can also be a worthwhile step in between high school and four-year college. Matt Varzino, a senior at the University of Tennessee, attended community college for two years following his high school graduation. The time he spent there was formative and allowed him to make well-considered decisions about his future. "I know my decision to go to community college was the right one, both professionally and financially," he told us. "My time spent there helped me decide what field I wanted to concentrate on, and I felt free to experiment with a variety of classes since credit costs were in the hundreds, not thousands, of dollars. I felt more prepared for university, and I would recommend that people who are not sure of their interests, or who simply want to save money, do at least a year of community college classes."

Why are there not more high school guidance counselors promoting community colleges? One reason is that they do not want to appear to discriminate against low-performing students. Many people think that a four-year bachelor's degree is the key to prosperity, even though a two-year degree might be a better choice.

Community colleges help students gain knowledge necessary to transfer to four-year institutions, if they so choose. They also offer students the possibility of a two-year associate degree that can pave the way to a wide range of careers, including many that offer high pay and steady employment. For those who need an extra boost, remedial courses at community college can help develop basic skills, especially in math and writing. By accepting transfer students and focusing on practical skills needed for work—which are especially valuable to students who have been adversely affected by recent economic trends—community colleges can boost economic mobility.

Data from Florida show that if low-income and low-achieving students attain credentials in high-return fields, such as health care, they can find well-paying jobs, earning approximately $45,000 when they enter the workforce and $60,000 after seven years.[37] Young people need to gain training that will propel them to worthwhile careers.

Many high-return fields, such as health care, computer programming, building trades, and protective services, are open to community college students with relatively low high school GPAs. Community colleges play a major role in increasing the earnings of students who would have difficulty boosting their career prospects by completing the four-year programs required to enter high-return fields.

Jobs in health-care services, such as physician's assistants, occupational therapists, and nurses, are growing. The Bureau of Labor Statistics projects that health-care occupations will see the most job growth during the next decade, to 15.6 million, or a 10.8 percent increase.[38] Throughout the recession and the sluggish recovery, jobs in health services have never declined. This is partly due to the aging population and to the fact that people cannot predict when they are going to fall ill; unlike money for discretionary purchases, people do not know what they will spend on health care, or when.

There are many reasons to choose a two-year community college program over a four-year degree program, and the decision comes down to what is right for the individual, but government policies should not discourage what can be a very worthwhile investment. For about 35 percent of the cost of a attending a public, four-year, in-state college, and for about 10 percent or less of the cost of a private four-year college, community colleges offer a broad range of high-quality courses at a low tuition of about $3,200 annually.[39]

Community colleges are also widely distributed throughout America and offer classes at convenient times and locations, which makes it possible for students to live at home while working and maintaining family responsibilities. Altogether, 1,130 community colleges enroll 13 million students from a variety of educational backgrounds, from top students who cannot afford to attend a four-year college, to students who lack the credentials to get into a four-year college, to recent immigrants whose educational background might not have prepared them for a four-year college in the United States.

There are other solutions to the soaring cost of college besides embracing community colleges and technical schools. A few innovative start-up companies have found a way to help alleviate the student loan debt crisis. Upstart and Pave, a new breed of lenders, provide a technological platform that allows those with available money to invest in young people and their careers. With these lenders, investors are repaid through percentages of borrowers' monthly salaries for a period of up to 10 years. To determine individual rates, companies calculate likely future earnings based on university, major, grades, and professional experience. This rate—usually between 4 and 7 percent of income—enables investors to make informed decisions while weighing risk and return.

Investors have incentives to mentor those in whom they have a financial stake, which helps the young people succeed. The investors can offer personal advice and introduce their "investments" to professional networks. If the loan recipients' careers take off and their salaries increase, the investors' returns rise.

While investors might attempt to influence young peoples' careers, borrowers are free to choose any major or career after receiving the loans. Many borrowers find this opportunity liberating. The personal relationship to the investor can further motivate students to be successful.

If the income of a Pave borrower falls below 150 percent of the poverty line, he is allowed to defer repayment. Upstart's borrowers do not owe anything if they make less than $20,000 a year, but the repayment period can be extended. Whereas traditional student loans cannot be shed in bankruptcy, these pioneering loans can, if necessary.

With this business model, students have an economic incentive to choose degrees in high-return, in-demand majors such as engineering or computer science, because it means their repayment will be a lower percentage of their future salary.

With traditional student loans, the same rate of 4.66 percent applies to all undergraduates irrespective of field of study, test scores, or high school GPA. The across-the-board low interest rate is a type of economic misinformation that causes many students to choose a four-year college when they might have better options.

Those who stand to lose from Upstart, Pave, and others companies like them are the large financial institutions and underperforming colleges, which will use any hiccups the companies encounter as evidence for increased government regulation. In 10 years, more young people might finance their education or business through human-capital investments. However, if the government stifles innovators such as Upstart and Pave, students might miss valuable opportunities.

Innovation in higher education does not end with new financing models. College administrators and tenured professors are worried about the increasing popularity of massive open online courses (MOOCs). These offer free classes taught by some of the world's most renowned professors, who can teach tens of thousands of students at a time. While some aspects of college cannot be replaced with classes taught to thousands of people over the Internet, MOOCs can supplement higher education by reducing cost and increasing access. Courses that teach technical knowledge such as math and chemistry may be especially effective. Concerns about cheating and the educational value of the courses could be satisfied by setting up in-person testing and accredited content.

MOOCs are not a remedy for all the flaws in higher education, but they have the potential to make college more about learning and less about going deep into debt. They might especially excel at competency-based education, where knowledge is measured by what is learned rather than the time spent in a program. Students can study on their own time and learn at their own pace. The flexibility MOOCs offer can accommodate everyone from recent high school graduates wanting to learn skills and begin their careers as quickly as possible to older workers looking to study part time to keep their skills up-to-date. We should encourage further development in the MOOCs arena, not stifle innovation to protect an educational model that is centuries old.

The United States has more top universities than any other country in the world—74 in the 2014–2015 top 200 World University Rankings, developed by *Times Higher Education* magazine and Thomson Reuters. That is more than double the score of the country with the second most, the United Kingdom, which has 29 universities in the top 200. Germany has the third-highest, with 12, and Australia and the Netherlands are the only other countries with 10 or more. An examination of the 25 top-ranked universities makes American dominance even clearer. Of the top 25 universities, 17 (68 percent) are from the United States—Caltech, Harvard, Stanford, Massachusetts Institute of Technology, and Princeton are the top-ranked U.S. universities.[40] But it is vital to solve the funding problems so that young people can benefit from America's tremendous educational offerings.

Outstanding student loan debt is indeed a crisis. The job market for millennials remains weak, college costs continue to rise, and the government has yet to take meaningful action to reform higher education financing. Still, there is hope. A multitude of community colleges, innovative new financing models, cheaper online access to high-quality education, and the strength and diversity of American higher education all offer chances at successful reform that would go a long way toward turning around students' crushing debt burdens.

PART III

REGULATIONS THAT CRIPPLE THE YOUNG

I n Parts I and II, we described how millennials, even without the benefit of a good education that leads to well-paying jobs, will be forced to pay off the debt of prior generations. In Part III, we explain how labor-market regulations stifle the potential of new high school and college graduates, and we look at what can be done to bring these young people into the workforce. The challenge of paying off personal and government debt becomes that much more difficult when ever-more-complex regulations restrict the number of jobs available to new workers.

In Chapter 5, we show that industry cartels prevent young people from starting their own businesses. Excessive occupational licensing laws, which will affect 4 out of 10 workers, not only make it difficult for young Americans to put their skills to work, but they also drive up prices for services. Enacted in the name of public safety, most occupational licensing laws ensure anything but safety. Interior designers, florists, tree trimmers, hairstylists, and manicurists are all subject to varying degrees of licensing. These laws protect established tradespeople from competition, not the public from the dangers of mismatched curtains or drooping flowers. Occupational licensing protects the positions of privileged special interests at the expense of everyone else—especially the young.

In Chapter 6, we describe how wage regulations, while enacted with the admirable intention of helping the poor, have backfired as employers choose to hire fewer low-skill workers. Older, more-experienced workers whose skills create value above the minimum wage keep their jobs, while young people who are still gaining work experience find themselves with fewer employment prospects. High minimum wages effectively raise the first rung of the economic ladder to a level that is out of reach for many young workers.

Labor Department regulations restricting unpaid internships, also discussed in Chapter 6, have damaged the prospects of young people looking to gain experience in the workforce. With our education system in disarray and studies showing that internship experience is more important than choice of major to potential employers, résumé building is vital for young people. In the public sector, unpaid internships abound—Washington chooses to flout its own rules. But in the private sector, regulations force companies to limit the number of internships available, depriving young people of opportunities to develop their skills.

America cannot progress with a shrinking workforce that is thwarted from climbing the economic ladder. If we do not provide opportunities for today's young people, who lack the political organization to fight on their own behalf, economic growth will founder and future generations will pay a steep price.

CHAPTER 5

LICENSING REQUIREMENTS KEEP OUT THE YOUNG

Becky Maples always wanted to be a cosmetologist, but she was blocked from pursuing her dream by government bureaucracy. Now, instead of styling hair full time, she is working at an automotive warehouse outside Chicago. Becky studied cosmetology in high school and has been cutting and dying hair in a makeshift salon in her apartment since she was 15 years old. Even though friends and acquaintances love her work, her sense of style, and her friendly demeanor, the time and fees required to become a government-certified cosmetologist were too much for her.

Occupational licensing, the requirement that people pass tests to gain government permission to work, is making it harder for young people to begin their careers. By keeping young people out of certain industries, or by making it prohibitively expensive and time-consuming for them to work, occupational licenses increase costs for all Americans and limit opportunity for those looking to enter the field of their choice.

Some limits on work seem specifically directed at the young. In Virginia, those who trained yoga instructors had to be certified by a state board of older bureaucrats who probably knew nothing about the recent yoga craze.[1] A similar Nevada law restricts the teaching of how to apply makeup.[2] These cases not only hurt those who want to teach—they affect the young people who want to learn a skill and put it to work.

Those who want to be computer-repair technicians in Texas must obtain a private-detective license because of overstated concerns about security.[3] Young people grew up with computers; their parents and grandparents often already ask them to help organize and repair their home computers—without a private-detective license. Absurd laws such as this make it illegal for young people to share their knowledge and earn some money while doing so.

Tour guides in cities such as Charleston, South Carolina; Savannah, Georgia; and New Orleans must gain certification before the government allows them to earn money by walking and talking—two rights clearly protected by the American Constitution.[4] All of these cities are known for their number of colleges and universities, but now, unless they spend their limited time and money getting a license, students cannot earn a salary to pay for their education by showing tourists around on the weekend.

The case of Christian Alf shows that many state licensing boards are looking out for their own interests, not the public's.[5] The Arizona teen started a business repairing holes in his neighbors' roofs to protect them from roof rats. All Christian needed to do this was a ladder, chicken wire, and a staple gun. He charged $30 for his service and quickly drew attention from interested homeowners—and envious pest-control companies. Christian was doing what pest-control companies charged hundreds of dollars to do, so they sent a government agent to his front door to demand that he stop providing unlicensed pest control to his neighbors. One problem: Christian was performing handyman work. He was not using any chemicals or traps that could possibly provide rationale for mandatory training and government certification.

The Institute for Justice, a public-interest law firm that defends individuals' rights to earn a living, stepped in to defend Christian. Arizona's Structural Pest Control Commission stepped back under the weight of public pressure, finally allowing Christian to provide his neighbors with valuable services, free of government harassment.

Young people are hardest hit by the effects of occupational licensing, along with the poor. Costly, time-consuming entry barriers limit the competition that would keep prices down, so consumers pay higher prices while also being excluded from job opportunities.

Becky Maples had little recourse because every state and the District of Columbia licenses cosmetologists. The average required education and experience for cosmetologists takes more than a year to complete. Additionally, multiple exams and hundreds of dollars in fees are required.[6] Becky is clearly a talented hair stylist, as she continues to cut and dye hair in her apartment on nights and weekends when she has breaks from her work at the factory. Someone with her skill level, qualifications, and eager customers should not have to pay for government approval in order to work. As occupational licensing laws become ever more numerous and complex, the freedom of young people to choose their occupations is increasingly stifled.

One type of government regulation that hits particularly close to home for millennials is the excessive hurdles placed in the way of craft breweries. While large, established beer producers were busy competing over whose beer was colder or whose can or bottle had the best airflow system, thousands of smaller American breweries were competing on taste and variety. Consumers are thirsty for craft beer: Sales jumped 17 percent in 2013, while overall beer sales decreased 2 percent.[7] Last year there were 2,822 breweries operating in the United States, the largest number since the 1870s, according to Generation Opportunity president Evan Feinberg. The industry provides more than 1 million direct jobs in the United States,[8] and the rise of craft breweries injects some much-needed excitement and competition into the American beer industry.

The threat of increased competition, however, does not sit well with larger breweries, so they are hiding behind excessive regulations that keep new brewers out. One example of regulations that increase the costs of bringing beer to markets is the "three-tier" distribution system. This Prohibition-era system requires that alcohol suppliers, wholesalers, and retailers remain separate. If small brewers want to get their beer to customers, they have to pay larger companies to distribute and sell it. Having an unnecessary middleman leads to higher costs for both craft breweries and their customers.

The barriers to selling craft beer are not only a matter of antiquated distribution laws. It takes an average of 188 days—over half a year—for a brewery to navigate its way through the federal application process. In October 2014, it took an average of 112 days for the Alcohol and Tobacco Tax and Trade Bureau to process an application to start a new brewery.[9] Gaining approval for a beer's formula takes 60 days,[10] and the label-approval process adds another 16 days.[11]

On top of the federal regulations, state-level laws add even more hurdles. Brewers in Virginia, for example, must comply with about 12 separate regulatory steps before selling beer—levels expected in Venezuela or China, not the United States.[12] These barriers to entry are subjective and susceptible to special-interest influence. Virginia regulators can deny a brewing license for a number of arbitrary reasons. These include the brewer's being "physically unable to carry on the business" or not a person of "good moral character and repute," a failure to demonstrate the "financial responsibility sufficient to meet the requirements of the business," or an inability to "speak, understand, read, and write the English language in a reasonably satisfactory manner." A regulator can even deny a license if he decides that there are sufficient brewers in the area and that additional ones would be "detrimental to the interest, morals, safety, or welfare of the public."[13]

These regulations not only keep good beer from consumers, but they also create formidable barriers to entry into a growing industry. This protection of large, established interests at the expense of new, smaller businesses is a problem we can see throughout the American economy.

The government-imposed limits on work extend far beyond the professional fields of medicine, law, and accounting—fields for which the need for a license is commonly accepted. About 1 in 3 occupations requires a government license or certification, and nearly 40 percent of U.S. workers will need to get government permission to work at some point in their lives.[14] By contrast, less than 5 percent of the workforce needed a license in the early 1950s.

In its report "License to Work," the Institute for Justice evaluated 102 low- and moderate-skill licensed occupations. On average, these licensed workers are required to spend nine months in education or training, pass an exam, and pay more than $200 in fees, all in the name of public safety.[15] One-third of the licenses take more than a year to earn. About 50 of the occupations studied offer the possibility of entrepreneurship, meaning they can lead to small-business creation. This suggests that licensing laws affect both an individual's ability to get a job and to create jobs for others.

The time and financial burdens of getting a license vary considerably across states. This variation shows that public safety cannot be the main concern of lawmakers, despite their claims to the contrary. Although 10 states require four months or more of training for manicurists, Alaska demands only about three days and Iowa about nine days. If it really takes more than four months to learn how to manicure nails without injuring customers, why do 40 states have much shorter requirements?

Few occupations are universally licensed. Out of the 102 occupations studied by the Institute for Justice, only 15 are licensed in 40 states or more. If working in these occupations truly posed dangers to the public, one would expect them to require licensing in every state, or at least in most states. Seven states require a license for tree trimming, yet the other 43 do not suffer from an epidemic of poorly trimmed greenery.[16] Nevada requires almost two and a half years of education and training to work as a barber, but Wyoming requires 175 days.[17] Why does a barber need four times more training in Nevada than in Wyoming—are men's haircuts of a much higher quality in Nevada?

The difficulty of starting work does not seem to be correlated with health or safety risks. Interior designers, who have some of the most onerous licensing requirements in the United States, need to pay an average of $364 in fees and clock six years of experience to obtain a license.[18] This harmless occupation (unless ugly sofas and armchairs pose a danger) is licensed only in Florida, Nevada, Louisiana, and the District of Columbia.

On the other hand, bus drivers, who are licensed in every state, can begin working for less than $100 in training fees and 90 days' experience. The health and safety of the public is directly affected by the work of emergency medical technicians, yet 66 other occupations face greater average licensure burdens. States consider an average of 33 days of training and two exams enough preparation for EMTs, but they apparently think that interior designers need 70 times more training. It should not require more training to become a government-approved interior designer than a bus driver or an EMT.[19]

Louisiana is the only state to license florists. Florists pose no evident danger to the public, and licensing does not always improve the quality of the work. Professor Dick Carpenter of the University of Colorado examined flower arrangements and found no difference in perceived quality between licensed and unlicensed florists.[20] Still, the pass rate for Louisiana florist certification is lower than the pass rate for the Louisiana Bar exam. This is undoubtedly because those judging the floral arrangements are established florists who would prefer not to face increased competition. There should not be a test for something as subjective as tastes in flower arrangements, especially a test administered by the test taker's future competitors.

The strictness of occupational licensing laws is correlated with the rate of youth unemployment. The unemployment rate in 2012 for 16- to 19-year-olds in the 10 states with the least burdensome licensing requirements was 19 percent, compared with 27 percent for the states that have the most burdensome requirements. For those ages 20 to 24, these numbers were 11 percent and 14 percent, respectively.[21] The difference in licensing requirements might be one factor contributing to the wide variation in youth unemployment rates nationwide. Jobs that require licensing are among the most attractive to young workers, who are penalized by high barriers to entry.

Each year, Thumbtack.com, in partnership with the Kauffman Foundation, conducts a "Small Business Friendliness Survey" in which it asks small businesses nationwide to rate the business-friendliness of their state and local governments.[22] This comprehensive survey collects data from more than 12,000 diverse small-business owners to evaluate how business climates differ across the nation. The survey helps provide a clear picture of how policies directly affect entrepreneurs; it gives a real-world view not evident when analyzing government data alone.

Results show that small businesses care almost twice as much about licensing regulations as they do about taxes when rating the business-friendliness of their state or local government. Entrepreneurs are mainly focused on bringing their ideas and skills to market, and they want to use as much of their available, and often limited, resources to do so. Seeking government approval to go into business is a waste of their valuable time and money. This is why the burden of professional licensing regulations was found to be the only statistically significant non-demographic variable for predicting states' business environments. "The complexity, time-cost, and monetary expenditure of obtaining and keeping licenses and permits was the most important issue for small businesses when rating the friendliness of their states," wrote Thumbtack's chief economist, Jon Lieber, and its co-founder, Sander Daniels.[23]

Only 35 percent of Thumbtack's respondents thought they paid too much in taxes,[24] showing that respondents did not use the survey to complain about every difficulty they face. Many small-business owners identify professional licenses as their largest problem because these requirements have moved far beyond their initial goal of protecting public safety. Through sheer accumulation and the influence of special interests, they impede progress—to the detriment of the public.

Half of Thumbtack's respondents reported being subject to at least one professional licensing requirement.[25] Moreover, among those small businesses subject to special regulatory requirements, such as occupational licenses, the ease of compliance with these regulations was by far the best predictor of their view of how friendly to small business their respective states were.

Business environments differ substantially across the United States. Utah, Idaho, Kansas, Virginia, and Texas received the five highest ratings for having professional licensing requirements that were friendly to small business. Rhode Island, Connecticut, Illinois, Massachusetts, and California received the worst ratings.[26] It's no surprise that the average real GDP growth rate in 2013 was three times as high in the friendliest five states compared with the least-friendly five states (3 percent and 1 percent, respectively).[27]

By protecting established, older workers, the government's occupational licensing requirements make it hard for the young to enter the workforce as entrepreneurs—leaving them with fewer job opportunities. As the Thumbtack report states, "Over 99 percent of U.S. employer firms meet the Small Business Administration's definition of small businesses, and they account for nearly half of all private-sector employees. Over the past two decades, almost two-thirds of net new private-sector jobs have come from these small businesses."[28]

Ian Hathaway and Robert Litan of the Brookings Institution have shown that the decline in entrepreneurship is leading to the aging of American businesses. In 1992, 23 percent of firms had existed for 16 years. By 2011, this percentage had increased to 34 percent.[29] When there are fewer entrepreneurs and new market entrants, economist John Dearie convincingly argues, innovation lags and existing companies face lower pressure to improve quality or lower prices.[30] This is because new businesses are the main drivers of "disruptive" innovation that is, as Dearie puts it, "the sort of radical, rock-the-establishment innovation that re-makes the economic landscape, propels productivity and economic growth, and creates opportunity, wealth, and jobs for millions."[31] If licenses were required to design mobile phone apps, it is unlikely that

Snapchat, WhatsApp, or Instagram would ever have made it past government bureaucrats charged with protecting "public safety."

Occupational licensing raises the prices of goods and services for everyone, not only young people. When the number of businesses is artificially constrained by government licensing requirements, established businesses can charge higher prices. Academic studies have found that licensing increases prices by around 15 percent, depending on the occupation.[32] This may not seem much, but for an 18-year-old recent high school graduate who needs a haircut for a job interview, every dollar counts. Occupational licensing leaves 18-year-olds with fewer chances for employment while they are stuck paying more for goods and services.

Ironically, occupational licensing makes the public less safe, even though its justification is public safety. When prices are high because only a limited number of people work in a given industry, the cost of hiring those workers increases and customers have a greater incentive to take on potentially dangerous tasks, such as electrical work, on their own—sometimes with dangerous results. Occupational licensing creates an environment where only "Cadillac" levels of service are available for purchase; all others are illegal.

This finding is not new. In 1981, a study showed that rates of electrocution were higher in states that had the most burdensome licensing requirements for electricians.[33] When prices are too high, and the wait time is too long, consumers will take home repairs into their own hands, with predictably tragic results. Similarly, plumbing licensing makes people more likely to do their own work or use black-market labor, because costs are excessive. To give an extreme example of this, people in the Soviet Union resorted to black-market services for nearly everything because the supply of producers was so constrained.

With ridiculous requirements for harmless professions such as interior designers, tour guides, and florists, reasonable people would think that getting rid of the rules would be as simple as applying common sense. Overcoming onerous occupational licensing requirements is very difficult, however. Each licensing requirement is created by a strong special-interest group that will fight tooth-and-nail to protect its favored position. Under the guise of public safety, which is a bipartisan priority, millennials are left to the mercy of older (and richer) interests.

Perhaps no battle between entrenched interests and new competition is receiving more attention than that now being waged over ride-sharing companies. Among the main companies pushing to modernize the transportation industry are Uber, Lyft, and Sidecar. Uber and other ride-sharing services do not own the cars their drivers use; they provide the technological platform and support to connect drivers and riders. When people are looking for a ride, all they have to do is take out their smartphone and, with the touch of a button, request one. A few minutes later, the requested car pulls up and they are on their way. Once they reach their destination, they simply exit the car and payment is automatically taken care of, from the customer's credit card on file. Riders are encouraged to rate their trips, and drivers that fail to provide good service are removed from the companies' networks.

Besides the benefits to consumers, ride-sharing offers substantial benefits to drivers. If someone has a car that meets a company's standards and if they pass background and safety checks, they can be their own boss and start driving for that ride-sharing company. This entrepreneurial employment path is attractive to young people who are looking to earn extra money working part time, stay afloat while in between jobs, or start off a promising career; full-time Uber drivers' earnings exceed those of taxi drivers.[34]

Even though more than 100 cities worldwide allow consumers and drivers to embrace the benefits of ride-sharing services, some cities and states refuse to recognize that these services are different from taxi companies, and they are trying to regulate them as taxis or ban them outright. Anyone who has ridden with Uber or Lyft can easily tell that there are substantial differences between ride-sharing services and taxi companies: Finding rides is easier, the cars are nicer, the drivers are friendlier, and the prices are lower.

Governments across the country also refuse to recognize that applying regulatory standards that were codified before the Internet is no way to foster economic growth. Attempting to apply these regulations to ride-sharing companies is like trying to jam a square peg into a round hole. Passing one-size-fits-all protectionist regulations is precisely what triggered poor service, uncomfortable rides, and expensive bills in the taxi market and encouraged the rise of ride-sharing companies.

Taxi companies cannot compete on quality or price, so they are resorting to scare tactics and invoking the ever-familiar cry of public safety. The well-documented 2014 New Year's Eve tragedy in which a young girl was killed in San Francisco by a driver who was logged in to his Uber app is continually used as justification for further regulation. But Census data show that there are almost 11 million motor-vehicle accidents per year and 36,000 fatalities.[35] An isolated, unfortunate event might work as a rallying cry for entrenched taxi businesses that feel threatened by emerging competitors, but it does not show an increased risk to public safety.

Ride-sharing companies, of their own volition, already require background checks and insurance coverage, and they have vehicle-safety inspections and zero-tolerance policies on drugs and alcohol. This should come as no surprise: Injuring or killing customers is not a smart business model. If consumers did not feel safe, they would be hesitant to use ride-sharing services. While Uber, Lyft, and Sidecar all serve distinct purposes and cater to different customer bases, they share a common characteristic: the benefits they offer to drivers and consumers. Their drivers enjoy convenience and flexibility, and consumers benefit from lower prices and increased choice.

The desire to protect the profits of existing taxi drivers by locking out competition does not justify curtailing consumers' freedom to choose. It is also wrong to take away an avenue for employment that is especially appealing to young people. New technology will drive a stream of new services, and ride-sharing is only one example. If entrenched interests are allowed to defeat innovation, everyone else will lose.

When occupational requirements are lessened or eliminated altogether, some people are rightfully angry that they had to devote substantial amounts of time and money to get licenses while others can now compete without these costs. For example, taxi medallions in New York City have sold for more than $1 million. If drivers working with innovative ride-sharing companies are able to enter the market without paying this exorbitant amount, those who paid for medallions are at a competitive disadvantage. But people who were kept out of the market by occupational barriers were at an even larger disadvantage: They were not allowed to compete at all. There are more than 13,000 medallions in New York City. This might seem to be a lot, but anyone who has attempted to hail a cab after work or on a Saturday night knows that the number is not high enough. Keeping laws on the books that protect a chosen few at the expense of everyone else is neither fair nor smart economic policy.

Reimbursing some of the costs that existing practitioners had to pay is one solution that could make dissolving occupational licensing requirements a politically feasible possibility. This would be a large one-time cost, but it would pay off in the future when protected industries are opened up to increased competition from younger workers entering the market. Prices would fall, and innovative business models would thrive.

Melony Armstrong, the subject of the documentary *Locked Out: A Mississippi Success Story*,[36] experienced the harms of occupational licensing laws firsthand. When she decided she wanted to go into business as an African hair braider, she had no idea that a long, hard battle against the State Board of Cosmetology lay ahead. Her salon, Naturally Speaking, opened in Tupelo, Mississippi, in September 1999. Before Naturally Speaking opened, the hair-braiding salon closest to her hometown was in Memphis. Melony saw a business opportunity that would allow her to pursue her passion. From the time Melony decided she wanted to open a hair-braiding salon, it took her four years to realize her dream.

African hair braiding is a natural process that does not use any chemicals. For this reason, Melony saw no point in spending $10,000 and several years in a cosmetology school that would not teach her any of the skills she needed to braid hair. After the first of her many fights with the state government, she was able instead to earn a wigology license, which "only" required 300 hours of coursework—but not a single hour of braiding instruction.

As Melony's business expanded, she wanted to hire younger workers and train them so she could better manage the overwhelming demand for her services. In order to do that, however, she would have needed to complete another 3,200 hours of classes and apply for a cosmetology-school license. None of these hours in the classroom would have helped her learn how to braid hair, or how to teach braiding hair. In that time, Melony could have become licensed for all of the following occupations: EMT, police office, firefighter, paramedic, real estate appraiser, hunting education instructor, and ambulance driver—and she'd still have had 600 hours to spare.[37]

We asked Melony how these ridiculous requirements weighed on her, especially when she had to turn down young women who needed a chance to work. "When I first learned that I was not free to pursue my passion, I felt like I had hit a brick wall," she recalled. "I wondered whether I had made a mistake and if my effort, time, energy, and money invested were all for nothing. This was very similar to what I felt when I was legally prohibited from hiring the help I needed. The strong enthusiasm I had possessed about seeing my business grow and thrive began to weaken. The most difficult part about my ordeal was just thinking, *This just doesn't make sense.* All I was trying to do was braid hair and grow my business in a way that would afford my family financial freedom."

In 2004, Melony filed a lawsuit against Mississippi to end this madness. It was not easy to overcome the entrenched interests of the cosmetology board, but, on April 19, 2005, Mississippi's governor, Haley Barbour, freed hair braiders to practice their trade without the burdensome, pointless regulations. Now, all that is required to be a hair braider is a $25 payment and compliance with Mississippi's health and hygiene codes. There are now hundreds of entrepreneurs who followed Melony's example and own their own hair-braiding salons in Mississippi.

We asked Melony if she thought occupational licensing laws disproportionately harmed young people. "Yes, because most people seeking to enter the cosmetology field are going to be young people," she replied. "And if these kinds of laws are in place, after a while, these same young people who have a dream of entering this field, just to be shut out, will eventually let their dream die."

Once Mississippi finally updated its laws, Melony began hiring workers and expanding her business. One young worker she hired, Ebony Starks, was only 16. A few months after she began working, her father passed away. It was summer and Ebony was able to work full time and help her family financially cope with the loss. Ebony is 24 today, and she continues to braid hair at Naturally Speaking. She worked at the salon all through college breaks and now has a young daughter of her own. Prior to the reforms in 2005, Ebony's life might have been a lot more difficult, and for what? For the sake of protecting older, established salon owners? Melony sees embracing entrepreneurship as the way to prepare young people for our rapidly changing, 21st-century economy. The easiest way to do this, she says, is to get out of their way and allow them to apply their gifts and talents while they realize their dreams. We could not agree more.

Occupational licensing was originally intended to protect the public from unqualified lawyers and doctors. It has now morphed into a network of ubiquitous barriers that affect nearly 40 percent of American workers. This is what happens when special interests—such as state boards of cosmetologists, interior designers, taxi cartels, and pest controllers—manage to convince legislators that they deserve preferred treatment. America's economy is being damaged by occupational licensing, but the prospects of young people such as Ebony are being damaged most of all.

CHAPTER 6

BANNED FROM THE JOB MARKET

Robert Davis (not his real name), a successful entrepreneur in his late twenties, owns several frozen-yogurt shops in Kentucky. He wants to reduce poverty as much as anyone. But when we asked him about the employment effects of raising the minimum wage, especially the effects on other young people, he told us: "The minimum wage has the potential to really hurt the lowest-skilled workers that we hire. If the minimum wage crosses the $10-an-hour mark, we will focus on automation to remove the least efficient staff from our team."

Robert told us that it is the least skilled who will feel the negative consequences of raising the minimum wage, not those who are older and well established. "Those who are our top employees and shift leaders already make more than minimum wage, so they are safe," he said. "It is those who are not as experienced, and who do not provide $10 an hour worth of value to our company, who will be in real danger of losing their jobs. Just as with any other expenses, when something is not providing enough value, I simply stop buying it. Unfortunately, in the case of a higher minimum wage, doing so can artificially rob someone of an employment opportunity."

As Robert makes clear, raising the minimum wage discriminates against low-skill—often young—workers and reduces job opportunities for those who have few alternatives. With a minimum wage of $7.25, the hourly cost to the employer is about $8.50, including Social Security, worker's compensation, and unemployment insurance. This means that in the United States, people with skills that are worth less than $8.50 an hour are effectively barred from working. Advocates of raising the minimum wage are unintentionally pushing to make this group even larger.

The hourly federal minimum wage is now $7.25. In his State of the Union address in 2014, President Obama joined Democratic members of Congress in calling for an increase to $10.10, saying, "America deserves a raise." Some labor organizations and elected representatives have gone even further, proposing a "living wage" of $15 per hour.

States, counties, and cities can set their minimum wages higher—but not lower—than the federal rate. Twenty-one states have higher minimum wages than the federal wage. A few localities, such as Seattle, have passed a $15-per-hour minimum wage into law, due to take effect in three years for large companies (more than 500 employees) and in seven years for others. If only it were that easy to end poverty. Just require a higher wage, and everyone would be better off. Instead, a higher minimum wage squeezes young people and low-skill workers out of the labor market, damaging their job prospects until they can invest in more training.

Though often seen as an economic cure-all, minimum-wage requirements have the unfortunate side effect of decreasing economic opportunity for young workers. Over half of those who earn at or below the minimum wage are between the ages of 16 and 24.[1] Since the majority of those earning minimum wage are younger workers, increases in the minimum-wage rate affect them the most. The effect extends into the future, because young people often use minimum-wage jobs as stepping-stones to better careers.

Businesses do not have to pay the minimum wage; they always have the option to not pay people at all—by letting workers go or not hiring new applicants. When the minimum wage rises, employers try to replace their less-skilled workers with more-skilled ones or with machines. Some restaurants are installing tablets on their tables to substitute for waiters. (As well as not requiring wages, the tablets can increase orders because they have faster turnaround times and do not judge diners who order high-carbohydrate meals or several desserts.) The restaurant chain Chili's has just invested in 45,000 tablets for its 823 restaurants.[2] High school students and recent graduates might now be unemployed because Ziosk tablets have replaced them and they cannot compete with more-skilled workers for higher-paying jobs.

The reality is that very few workers in America make the minimum wage, because they rapidly move up the wage scale after attaining their first job. People who take minimum-wage jobs gain an entry to the world of work. Once they are in, they can keep climbing. It is not out of kindness that employers pay experienced employees more than the minimum wage; it is because that is the only way they can prevent employees from moving to other jobs. If people cannot get their first job, they cannot get their second job or their third.

During the recent recession, which coincided with an increase in the hourly minimum wage from $5.15 to $7.25 (from 2007 to 2009), the employment rate for young or low-skilled workers worsened disproportionately. In 2014, the teen unemployment rate was 20 percent, and the African-American teen unemployment rate was 33 percent. Although the total unemployment rate was 6.2 percent, the youth unemployment rate for people ages 20 to 24 was 11 percent.[3]

With the current minimum wage of $7.25 an hour, we are condemning teenagers to unemployed summers and a loss of the work skills that are necessary to develop human capital. Raising the minimum wage to $10.10—a 40 percent increase—would make it even harder for young people to gain real-world experience, because employers would be even less able to hire them. In 1974, in 1984, and even as recently as 1994, about 55 percent of 16- to 19-year-old workers sought employment. By 2004, the percentage had declined to 44 percent. Now, it is about 33 percent.[4]

This is not where America wants to be. Young people are discouraged by the lack of job opportunities and are dropping out of the workforce. Only 55 percent of workers ages 16 to 24 are participating in the labor force, compared with 66 percent in 2000, a decline of 11 percentage points in less than 15 years. To put this in perspective, if labor-force participation rates remained at 2000 levels, more than 4 million more young people would be in the workforce.[5]

If lower youth labor-force participation were explained by young people's spending more time in school, the decline would be less worrisome. More schooling would mean that young people were investing in skills for future high-paying jobs—good news for them and for the economy. But the percentage of 16- to 24-year-olds enrolled in high school, college, or university has barely changed over the past decade, rising from 56 percent to 57 percent.[6]

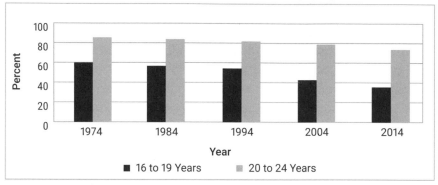

Male Labor-Force Participation Rate, by Age

Source: Bureau of Labor Statistics, Current Population Survey

People who want to raise the minimum wage (or raise the wage for tipped workers, which is now $2.13 an hour) generally have the best of intentions. They want workers to be better off. But fewer than 3 percent (3.3 million) of American workers earn the minimum wage,[7] and increases will damage job prospects for teens and unskilled workers, who already face elevated unemployment rates. The negative effects of increasing the minimum wage, however, would extend far beyond the 3 percent of workers who earn it.

If you were running a business, and the minimum wage rose from $7.25 to $10.10, you might lay off your least-skilled workers, or at least put a hold on low-skill hiring. Additionally, future workers would have to produce more, or you might decide to invest capital in labor-saving technology. You also might do less on-the-job training and hire more-experienced workers at the new, higher rate.

One reason that a low percentage of workers earn the minimum wage is that few workers stay at the minimum-wage level for long. In the United States, 1 in every 8 workers has held a job in McDonald's 750,000-person workforce. The company's high employee-turnover rate, of around 150 percent, is due to the high percentage of McDonald's employees who are aspiring young workers or people in transition periods between jobs seeking fast food employment to earn supplemental income or gain desired work experience.[8] Two-thirds of minimum-wage earners work part time, and the average income for households with a minimum-wage earner is more than $53,000.[9]

The question of how the minimum wage affects employment remains one of the most widely studied—and most controversial—topics in labor economics. Although some research concludes that raising the minimum wage has, at best, no employment effect,[10] most economists disagree and say that it destroys employment opportunities.

In a forthcoming paper in the *Industrial and Labor Relations Review*, David Neumark, a professor at the University of California at Irvine, writes that the strongest evidence linking unemployment to increases in the minimum wage comes from teenagers and other low-skill groups, without regard to industry.[11] He concludes, "The research record still shows that minimum wages pose a tradeoff of higher wages for some against job losses for others, and that policymakers need to bear this tradeoff in mind when making decisions about increasing the minimum wage."

In late 2013, 500 economists, including Nobel laureates Vernon Smith, Eugene Fama, Robert Lucas, and Edward Prescott, signed a letter opposing increases in the federal minimum wage.[12] One of the authors of this book (Diana) also signed the letter. "Although increasing wages through legislative action may sound like a great idea, poverty is a serious, complex issue that demands a comprehensive and thoughtful solution that targets those Americans actually in need," the letter stated.

This debate over the minimum wage highlights the problems of statistical analysis when interpreting complex economic situations. One reason that academics often find little overall change in employment when the minimum wage is raised is that minimum-wage workers constitute less than 3 percent of American workers; this makes it very challenging to tease out the effects on the aggregate economy of raising their wages.

Additionally, as Texas A&M University professor Jonathan Meer and MIT researcher Jeremy West argue, the effects of the minimum wage should be more apparent in new-job creation than in employment levels.[13] They show that it often takes time for effects of minimum-wage policy to be visible in employment levels, because these transitions are often slow. This is another reason studies often underestimate the negative employment effects of minimum-wage increases.

Nevertheless, while aggregate macroeconomic effects are hard to prove, evidence suggests that teens and low-skill workers are disproportionately affected by increases in the minimum wage.[14] When the minimum wage is increased, workers whose skills are below the new level are pushed out of the workforce or blocked from entering it. Young people who are seeking experience are put at a disadvantage. In earlier work, Neumark has shown that higher minimum wages have a particularly negative effect on African-American teens, whose unemployment rate now hovers around 33 percent.[15] Meer and West agree that the negative effects on job growth are concentrated in lower-wage industries and among younger workers. Making these unintended consequences worse is that these are the very people an increased minimum wage is supposed to help.

When policymakers and pundits pretend, as they often do, that increasing the rate would have no negative effects on inexperienced and low-skill workers, they are misleading the public. If minimum wages had no effect, why stop at $10.10? If an increase can lift people out of poverty without harming anyone else, it should make sense to raise the wage to $20.70 an hour, the average for nonsupervisory employees, or even higher.[16] The reality, of course, is that many people would not be employed if the hourly rate were this high—just as some will not be employed with an increase in the wage to $10.10. As is the case with many well-intentioned policies, the losers of higher-minimum-wage laws are those who lack political clout: the young or low-skilled.

In 2014, the Congressional Budget Office estimated that half a million employees would lose their jobs by 2016 if the hourly federal minimum wage rose to $10.10, although the report included the possibility that up to 1 million workers could become unemployed.[17] The report acknowledged the obvious—raising the minimum wage increases wages for some people, but, in exchange, prices inexperienced workers out of the labor market.

Some groups, such as the Service Employees International Union, want restaurants to pay fast food workers a minimum of $15 an hour, an increase of over 100 percent. As harmful as a minimum wage of $10.10 an hour would be, a level of $15 would be much worse. The leisure and hospitality industry is one of the prime employers of younger workers. With current levels of unemployment, and low levels of labor-force participation, young people need a lower minimum wage, not a wage floor that is doubled. In other words, teens need more options to work, not fewer.

Unions have been complaining that fast food chains are multinational corporations that make billions in profits, and that they can afford to pay more. They advocate minimum-wage increases because many union contracts are tied to the minimum wage. With increasing frequency, unions, under the guise of worker centers, are invading non-unionized workplaces and organizing strikes and protests in favor of increasing the minimum wage by more than 100 percent.

The United Food and Commercial Workers International Union (UFCW) funds worker centers such as the Restaurant Opportunities Centers United (ROC) and Jobs with Justice. ROC supports the "Fight for Fifteen" protests, which demand that restaurants pay an hourly minimum wage of $15. Jobs with Justice advocates a "living wage" of at least $12.50 an hour, along with health benefits and full-time positions for those who want them. Jobs with Justice and its affiliates received $230,000 from the UFCW in 2013.[18] Both of these wage levels would discourage firms from employing younger workers.

Washington policymakers are now also debating whether to increase the tipped minimum wage. Nearly 50 years ago, federal law created a lower minimum wage for workers who receive tips. It could not be less than 50 percent of the federal minimum wage. The Small Business Job Protection Act of 1996 detached tipped employees from future minimum-wage increases. This is why the tipped minimum wage is still $2.13 an hour, now 29 percent of the minimum wage.

Young people in particular value restaurant jobs with tips. When one of us (Jared) worked at a Thai restaurant during high school, he consistently earned more than $20 an hour on weekend nights. Waiters in Boston earn an average of $13.50 an hour,[19] according to the Labor Department, and waiters in northwest Florida earn $14.83 an hour. Waiter jobs are popular precisely because they offer the possibility of earning tips. Besides, if workers make less than $7.25 an hour, employers must make up the difference so that the worker makes the minimum wage.

Just as some states set minimum wages above the federal minimum, some states also set the tipped minimum above $2.13. Twenty-four states have a higher tip wage. An additional seven states, most of them in the

West, require waiters' base pay to be at least the state minimum wage. Some in Washington have proposed raising the hourly tipped minimum wage from $2.13 to 70 percent of the regular minimum wage. At today's current minimum, this would be $5.08 an hour. Then, the tipped minimum would rise with the regular minimum. But raising the tipped wage would have the same disadvantages as raising the regular minimum wage. Low-skill workers and teens who cannot find other jobs would have fewer work opportunities.

In 2014, Restaurant Opportunities Centers United organized a restaurant week in New York City to recognize eateries that have what it deems satisfactory employment practices. Partly because of the higher cost of labor, the average price of a burger and fries at the participating restaurants was $20.50. Many young people would prefer the McDonald's Dollar Menu or a $5 Footlong at Subway. A hungry student could eat four $5 Footlongs for $20 at Subway, whereas four burgers at an ROC-approved restaurant would bring the bill to $82. For young people just starting in their first job or making their way through school, cheap dining options are a necessity. Since labor costs are a major expense for restaurants, increases in wages that do not correspond with increased productivity raise prices for consumers.

Increases in the minimum wage or the tipped minimum wage do not affect all communities in the same way. In a large, diverse nation in which the median hourly wage can range from $10.81 in one locality to $37.59 in another, a one-size-fits-all federal minimum wage makes no sense.[20] Though the effects of a local minimum-wage hike are harmful, a national minimum-wage hike would be disastrous.

Most who want a higher minimum wage argue in support of increasing the federal, not the state or local, minimum wage. Twenty-nine states and the District of Columbia have a rate above the federal level. The commonly proposed federal rate of $10.10 is above Washington State's level of $9.47 an hour—the highest state-level minimum wage in the nation in 2015.[21] Labor-market conditions and cost of living differ throughout the country, as we see in the fact that it is very difficult to statistically measure the real effects of minimum-wage increases. There is no reason a worker in rural Alabama should have to be paid at the same rate as someone in downtown Boston.

States and cities have not been reluctant to pass minimum-wage increases on their own: Twenty-nine states have minimum wages set at hourly rates above the federal level. Just two states have rates below the federal minimum, while five additional states have no state minimum-wage laws. In practice, employers in these states must still pay the federal minimum wage in spite of the lower state laws.[22]

Five states (Connecticut, Hawaii, Maryland, Massachusetts, Vermont) and Washington, D.C., have voted to raise their minimum wages to $10.10 an hour or higher in the coming years.[23] All the jurisdictions that are in the process of raising their minimum wage to $10.10 an hour or higher have something in common: They are among the top 12 states in terms of cost of living. Hawaii has the highest living costs in the nation; Connecticut, the second; Washington, D.C., the third.[24] These places are better suited to absorb the negative consequences of raising the minimum wage than are states with a lower cost of living. When wages and costs of living are high, minimum-wage increases are not as large of a shock to labor markets as in places with a lower wage and cost of living.

The 12 states with the highest cost of living all have a minimum wage above the federal level. Alternatively, eight of the 12 states with the lowest cost of living have a minimum wage at or below the federal level. After successful November 2014 ballot initiatives to raise the minimum wage, Arkansas and Nebraska join Michigan and New Mexico as the outliers— of the 12 lowest-cost-of-living states, these four now have a minimum wage higher than the federal level.

The states that would be most affected by the proposed federal minimum-wage increase are Alabama, Arkansas, Florida, Idaho, Louisiana, Mississippi, Oklahoma, South Carolina, Tennessee, Texas, and West Virginia. In these 11 states, more than a quarter of workers earn below the proposed hourly minimum wage of $10.10. They have the lowest wages in the country. Mississippi would be the hardest hit, with a quarter of its workers earning $9.34 per hour or less.[25]

Different localities that add to their own fiscal problems by raising their minimum wage above the federal level should be prepared to live with the consequences. If the wages cause residents and businesses to move out of state, reducing tax revenue and increasing unemployment rates and pension liabilities, cities have only themselves to blame.

If the minimum wage helped low-income workers, we would expect that senators and representatives in Congress representing these states would be outspoken in their support for a minimum wage. But no, these members are against such an increase because they know that raising the minimum wage has unintended consequences for those they represent. In 2007, American Samoa, for instance, lobbied *not* to have the U.S. mainland minimum wage, because such a wage would harm the island's economic development and destroy its tuna industry.[26]

In 49 out of the 50 states, at least 10 percent of workers would be affected by a $10.10 minimum wage. Alaska is the only state in which the 10th-income-percentile wage (which is the wage below which 10 percent of workers fall) is more than $10.10 an hour.[27]

Many Washington politicians seem unable to realize the economic tradeoffs that would result from raising the federal minimum wage. Yet they understand the negative consequences they would feel if they were forced to pay their office interns the minimum wage. Reasonable people might assume that legislators who support raising the federal minimum wage would pay their employees the current minimum wage of $7.25 or their proposed level of $10.10. But, once again, our leaders in Washington are telling Americans to do as they say, not as they do.

In the 113th Congress, Senate Committee on Health, Employment, Labor, and Pensions chairman Tom Harkin (D., Iowa), who has since retired, and Representative George Miller (D., Calif.), the ranking member on the House Education and Workforce Committee, sponsored legislation to increase the federal minimum wage and tipped minimum wage. The bill gained more than 200 co-sponsors.

Surprisingly, neither Harkin nor Miller paid their congressional interns, and the double standards extend to the other sponsors. The Employment Policies Institute found that 96 percent of the sponsors did not pay any of their interns. This means, as the EPI report stated, that "the same members of Congress who are supporting a 40 percent wage hike on private-sector employers are simultaneously failing to provide any wages to their own employee interns."[28] No surprise—there appears to be a high level of hypocrisy in congressional offices. These senators and representatives would most likely defend their actions by claiming that the benefits they offer to interns justify the lack of pay. Clearly this is what the young people who take the internships believe, or they would not have applied for the highly competitive positions.

Absent their support for increasing the federal minimum wage, members of Congress are justified in offering unpaid internships. Unpaid internships, in Congress and elsewhere, benefit interns. For the same reasons, minimum-wage jobs are often worthwhile investments for young people. Internships and entry-level jobs provide real-world experience, which leads to stronger résumés and better jobs in the future. Students can also try out different workplaces to see what sort of work best suits their skills and interests.

"My first internship wasn't particularly exciting—working at the city and helping with random projects, so it wasn't too structured," millennial Katya Margolin told us. "But it was professional experience, an opportunity to see the real world and learn to interact with older professionals. My second internship was the following summer, before my senior year, and it was fantastic. I loved the subject and the experience, and I executed a project of my own that was intellectually and creatively fulfilling to me, and I did very well. To this day, I still seek a job that will give me the feeling and fulfillment that project gave me."

No one forces students into unpaid internships. Quite the opposite— unpaid internships on Capitol Hill are difficult to obtain. Interns are coming to the Hill to learn and gain experience. They are making investments in education that will pay off in their future careers. Requiring employers to pay wages above the value that employees provide limits options for young people to make investments in their human capital.

Higher-minimum-wage supporters in Washington could also argue that if they were forced to pay their interns, they would not be able to hire as many young people. How can they fail to realize that businesses will face these same disincentives if they are forced to pay more?

The government allows members of Congress, along with other Washington agencies and nonprofits, to offer unpaid internships, but it prohibits for-profit corporations from doing so unless they meet stringent, unworkable requirements.[29] Under guidelines published by the Labor Department in 2010, a private-sector internship can be unpaid if it is deemed "educational," whatever that means. It must benefit the intern, who must not displace regular staff. The employer cannot benefit from the intern's presence. These requirements do not lead to meaning-ful internships. Employers have to pay thousands of dollars for what are effectively training programs, or students have to pay colleges to partici-pate in unpaid internships.

These guidelines have resulted in frivolous lawsuits filed against companies offering worthwhile internships in in-demand fields. CBS and *The Late Show with David Letterman*, for instance, had a class-action complaint from previous interns filed against them in September 2014.[30] The plaintiffs are seeking all the compensation they would have earned if their internships had been paid, plus interest and legal costs. These interns knew that the internships were unpaid before they accepted the offers—they were applying for them to gain valuable experience in the highly competitive television industry. Opening up companies to poten-tial lawsuits such as this one does nothing to promote hands-on work experience for young people.

Some critics of unpaid internships support a mandate requiring internships to be accompanied by college credit. One problem with this, though, is that interns frequently must pay tuition to get college credit—a worse solution than an unpaid internship alone. At George Washington University in Washington, D.C., for example, a student could pay up to $12,175 in tuition just to be in a position to accept an unpaid intern-ship offer.[31] For a public four-year college, the average tuition cost of an unpaid internship is over $2,000 before financial aid.[32] Why not let students participate in unpaid internships and use their money to learn calculus, statistics, or computer programming? We should praise young people who want to spend their summers as unpaid interns, not pun-ish them. They realize that they have something to learn that cannot be taught at college.

The negative consequences of prohibitions against unpaid internships are real. Students lose the chance to combine part-time paid work with an internship, and they miss out on the opportunity to see a workplace up close and make valuable contacts that might lead to a permanent job. Take Sammy Page (not his real name), a philosophy major at a top university who plays the guitar and violin, composes, has his own band, and wants a career in the music business. After submitting countless applications, Sammy was overjoyed when he was offered an unpaid internship with a major New York City record company. But the company said he had to receive academic credit from his university in order for them to offer him the internship. Sammy's university, like many others, does not grant credit for summer internships. His dean offered to write to the record company, saying the school supported the internship. That offer was not enough for the record company to be in compliance with government regulations.

The record company suggested that Sammy enroll in a community college that would grant him course credit for the summer. Sammy would be required to pay money, which he does not have, to do this. Instead of gaining valuable career experience, he was left playing his violin on the streets of New York City and studying recording techniques on his computer.

These limitations will continue to affect Sammy far into the future. After spending a summer out of work, he may face hurdles to landing a job in the music industry. The ban on unpaid internships harms job prospects. Economists ran an experiment in which they created 9,400 fake résumés and sent them to employers in the fields of banking, finance, insurance, management, marketing, and sales. They found that internship experience on the résumé has a greater effect on hiring than does the applicant's academic major.[33] A student is more likely to get a job in banking if he interned at a bank than if he majored in a related field, such as finance. That is because the employer sees the internship as a measure of interest and experience.

Auburn University's Richard Seals, one of the study's authors, told the *Wall Street Journal*, "There is a huge return, even years later, to internships."[34] That is why young people compete to get them rather than taking a summer off or relaxing on weekdays during the school year.

It is unacceptable that the government has exempted itself and its supporters from the very rules it forces others to follow. Washington understands basic economics when the negative consequences of laws and regulations affect its own. If members of Congress would apply to the country as a whole the same reasoning they use when making decisions that affect their staffs and families, many destructive economic policies would not be voted into law.

Returning to the minimum wage, localities show even broader variation in prices than do states. Seattle decided in mid-2014 to raise the city's minimum wage to $15 an hour, one of the highest in the nation; this matches the one approved by voters in 2013 in nearby SeaTac,

Washington. Seattle's new minimum wage is a 58 percent increase from Washington State's 2015 rate of $9.47, and it will be indexed for inflation in the future. The phase-in schedule depends on the number of employees in a firm and whether or not the firm offers health insurance, but for some the minimum wage will rise to $15 an hour as soon as 2017.

With a $15 minimum-wage floor, Seattle can say good-bye to many of its young low-skilled workers. The city government must have decided it can do without them because of the city's highly skilled workforce—Amazon.com and Nordstrom are just two of the corporations headquartered in downtown Seattle, in addition to several medical and biotechnology firms. Competition for the few remaining low-skill jobs that remain in the city will increase, with medium-skilled, experienced workers winning out over low-skilled, mainly young, workers trying to reach the first rung of the career ladder.

People working in restaurant, personal-care, or building-maintenance jobs will be most affected. These three occupational categories each have median hourly wages below $15, and they account for 14 percent of employment in the Seattle-Tacoma-Bellevue metropolitan area (not to be confused with Seattle proper).[35] This group is too small and too young to hold much political sway, although they will bear the brunt of the minimum-wage increase.

In addition to young workers, customers in Seattle will undoubtedly feel negative effects as well. The Congressional Budget Office estimates that an increase in the federal minimum wage to $10.10 an hour would burden the U.S. private sector with $15 billion in additional costs.[36] More often than not, these costs get passed on to customers in the form of higher prices—and higher prices disproportionately hurt those with low incomes. Downtown Seattle workers, even if they can keep their jobs, should still expect to see an uptick in the price of lunches and after-work drinks.

Seattle shows why Washington has no business in raising the minimum wage. States and localities with different costs of living are making decisions to raise their minimum wages without any prompting or mandates from the federal government. Seattle can always reverse its flawed course, and the negative effects it suffers will be confined to a metropolitan area, not spread unevenly throughout the country. It is much harder for Washington to change its laws.

Seattle is not alone in looking to raise its minimum wage to unseen levels. After a successful November 2014 ballot initiative, San Francisco is following suit. A study by the San Francisco Office of Economic Analysis estimates that the city's minimum-wage increase to $15 an hour will cause the loss of more than 15,000 jobs by 2019.[37] This is 2 percent of the city's overall employment, and half the decline in employment would come from the food-services and retail-trade industries.

Both San Francisco and Seattle have higher average hourly wages than does the overall United States. The average wage is 45 percent higher in San Francisco and 27 percent higher in Seattle. Cost of living is also far above the national average in both these cities—64 percent higher in San Francisco and 21 percent higher in Seattle.[38] For these reasons, a $15-per-hour minimum wage might not have as large of an effect on workers in affluent Seattle and San Francisco.[39]

Other areas, however, are in a different economic environment. In Myrtle Beach, South Carolina, food preparation is the largest major employment field, and its median hourly wage is $11.52,[40] about half of Seattle's, where less than 8 percent of employment is in food preparation and the median hourly wage is $22.43. Federal laws should not force both cities to have the same minimum wage.

The federal government allows cities and states to raise their minimum wage above the federal floor. Why not drop the federal minimum wage and allow states and cities to set whatever wage floor they desire? The mayor and city council members of Myrtle Beach know the needs of their constituents better than President Obama does. Minimum wages inflict harm wherever they exist, but a federal minimum-wage floor is the most economically destructive.

Raising the minimum wage, while attractive as a political talking point, does real damage to employment. The amount of damage inflicted varies based on the skills and experience of workers and where they live. As with most other things in life, a one-size-fits-all standard does not work. When the minimum wage is too high, young people cannot get jobs. Their human capital is arguably their most important asset. When the first step to a career is too high to reach, young people are left behind. Rather than raising the minimum wage and limiting unpaid internships, Washington should repeal its well-intentioned but destructive laws.

PART IV

WHERE TO FROM HERE?

Time and time again, Washington has shown its unwillingness to tackle the main moral and economic issues facing the nation. The longer our leaders delay, the harder it will be to undo the damage wrought by economic policies that are betraying America's young. The problems facing America and its young are steep, but they are surmountable. Instead of caving in to special interests, Washington can work to adopt the commonsense reforms described in the previous chapters. These include halting the explosion of entitlement-driven debt, repealing the most destructive aspects of the ACA, fostering more school choice, reining in the cost of college, eliminating most occupational licenses, and repealing the federal minimum wage. All of this will require greater political engagement from young people and general recognition by the entire population of the scope of America's mistreatment of its young.

Addressing the rapidly expanding maze of federal and state-level regulations is another necessary step we must take to free the American economy and its workers. When entrepreneurs and successful businesses are strangled by heavy-handed regulations that do little more than create a maze of red tape, the economy is constrained. We cannot accept as normal and pass on to the next generation an economic growth rate of 2 percent.

When a nation systematically runs up bills, leaving them to be paid by the young, it creates a class of disinherited—people whose futures are determined before they are born, before they go to school, before they start their first job. Chapter 7 expands on how Washington can shift course, and Chapter 8 presents conclusions.

————— ● —————

CHAPTER 7

RECLAIMING THE DISINHERITED GENERATION

The explosive growth of programs that benefit the old at the expense of the young is only one aspect of the myriad government policies that disadvantage America's younger generation. Not only are the young forced to pay for their parents' health care and retirement benefits, but they also encounter an education system that bankrupts them and leaves them far behind their peers in other countries. When young people leave school, they face a hostile job market littered with government regulations. These problems are systemic, and only a radical shift in politics and the policies they produce can turn the tide.

Why do politicians refuse to respond to the mistreatment of so many young Americans? Why is it so difficult to alter the egregious policies that keep young people unemployed, uneducated, and liable for trillions of dollars in unfunded promises?

In Washington, D.C., and in state capitols around the country, entrenched interests protect the old, who have had the time and resources to build up a powerful political apparatus. Washington dare not take on the American Association of Retired Persons, one of the largest interest groups in the country, and change the unsustainable trajectory of entitlement programs. Rather than modify the benefit structure of Social Security to defend its solvency, the AARP chooses to protect generous benefits for today's retirees and disregards the future. To accomplish this, the AARP deploys its vast lobbying machine. The organization spent $25 million on lobbying in the 2012 presidential-election cycle and more than $16 million in the 2014 midterm-election cycle. Based on money spent lobbying, the AARP consistently ranks in the top 1 percent of organizations tracked by the Center for Responsive Politics.[1]

Medicare, which will become insolvent sooner than Social Security, is defended by its own interest groups, such as the National Committee to Preserve Social Security and Medicare. The Committee is rated as a "heavy hitter" in terms of political spending and is described by the Center for Responsive Politics as one of the largest donors to federal elections since 1990.[2]

At the state level, public-sector unions keep in place defined-benefit pension plans that promise generous payouts to today's retirees at the expense of everyone else. While union bosses are free to negotiate favorable contract terms with the politicians that they bankroll, critical parties are left out—taxpayers and those who will be responsible for paying unfunded liabilities in the future.

Many other interest groups lobby for policies that harm young people, such as minimum-wage hikes and other labor-market regulations that prevent the unskilled from entering the job market. Occupational licensing laws stay in place thanks to the efforts of those who already hold those licenses and want to defend their favored positions. Teachers' unions protect the jobs of poor educators and stand in the way of meaningful education reforms that would greatly benefit students and younger, more effective teachers.

Proportionately, the young do not vote. Seniors, though, take voting as seriously as a job. In the 2012 election, turnout among those ages 65 and older was 72 percent, compared with 41 percent for 18- to 24-year-olds.[3] The gap between voter turnout for the young and old increased from 15 percentage points in 1964 to 32 percentage points in 2012. Given the indirect costs imposed on young people by many government policies, these statistics are surprising, though many young people might not realize how the policies are directly affecting them. "Our generation has grown up with full acceptance of crushing national debt," one frustrated 25-year-old told us. "We might not care as much as we should because we have never known life without it."

One reason young people choose not to vote is that many feel alienated by America's two-party system. Two-thirds of millennials perceive government to be inefficient and wasteful. The last five years have left a sour taste in young people's mouths—back in 2009 only 4 in 10 millennials saw government as inefficient and wasteful. Now, only 18 percent of millennials believe regulators have the public's interest in mind, while 63 percent think that regulations benefit special interests. [4]

Over 60 percent of millennials describe themselves as socially liberal, yet 73 percent favor allowing people to have private Social Security accounts. Additionally, 64 percent say that cutting government spending would help the economy, and 59 percent say cutting taxes would grow the economy. On the whole, young voters find themselves politically unaligned, as they tend to be socially liberal and fiscally conservative. This could help explain why millennials appear politically disengaged and why they often choose to remain independent.

How can we change Washington's direction in order to paint a brighter future for America's next generation? Certain programs must be reformed, and certain laws must be changed or repealed. The steps we must take are not politically easy, but each is necessary.

Rather than papering over budget holes and continuously postponing reform, Congress must critically examine its spending every year and cut out waste, such as redundant, ineffective job-training programs, government-guaranteed loans to politically connected companies, and costly subsidies to favored industries.

Perhaps the easiest way to begin digging out of this debt is regulatory reform. America's regulatory state has expanded steadily since the 1970s. In 1975, the Code of Federal Regulations was 71,224 pages. By 2013, the number of pages had grown to more than 175,000.[5] The sheer quantity of government red tape makes it impossible for ordinary Americans to know whether they are breaking the law while working to start or maintain a business.

The Mercatus Center at George Mason University found a 28 percent increase in federal regulatory restrictions from 1997 to 2012.[6] Researchers analyzed the content of regulatory text to measure the number of command words such as "shall" or "must." This provides a clearer picture of Washington's regulatory labyrinth, because some regulations ramble on for pages with few restrictions while others are short but filled with many binding rules.

These commands from Washington bureaucrats have real-world effects. Entrepreneurs are focused on bringing their ideas and skills to market, and want to use all their available, and often limited, resources to do so. Forcing potential or current small-business owners to spend time and money on regulatory compliance that they could use for expanding their businesses inflicts substantial costs on the overall economy.

Number of Pages in the Code of Federal Regulations

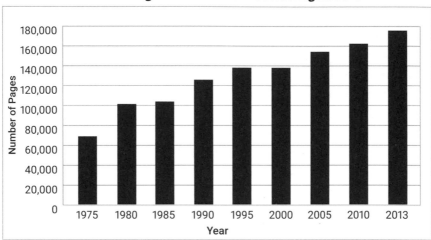

Source: "Code of Federal Regulations Page Breakdown—1975 through 2013," Office of the Federal Register, 2014

Cutting back on government regulations that do little more than increase the size of bureaucracies and protect politically connected interests should be a bipartisan priority. Not only is it unfair to single out individuals for adverse treatment, but an overzealous regulatory state also slows economic growth. Putting in place sunset provisions (requirements that regulations fall off the books without explicit reauthorization by the legislature) is a sensible remedy that would rid America of many of its most pointless and harmful regulations. Currently, most regulations are set on autopilot; as with entitlement programs, they take on lives of their own.

Regulatory growth in the second half of the 20th century lowered economic growth by an average of 2 percent per year. If the United States had kept its regulatory state at 1949 levels, GDP would now be about three and a half times higher, and every American would be about $130,000 richer.[7] The World Bank, in a comparison of economic performance in nations around the world, reports that heavily regulated countries experience slower economic growth.[8] Increased economic growth from regulatory reform would allow the government to collect more revenue to help balance the budget or pay down the debt, all without any increases in tax rates.

While the benefits of regulatory reform are widespread, the costs of burdensome regulations disproportionately affect those with low incomes. This means that most young people are bearing the weight of regulations, along with all other Americans who are living within limited means. Federal regulations cost six to eight times more as a share of earnings for low-income households compared with what high-income households pay.[9]

Simply stated, with the right approach to regulatory reform, the United States can grow, at least partly, out of its fiscal problems. But it is impossible to right America's fiscal ship if Washington does not enact long-term reforms to entitlement programs to make them sustainable in the long run. With Social Security and Medicare projected to cost a combined 12 percent of GDP by 2035, up from 8 percent in 2013 and 6 percent in 2010, we cannot allow Washington to delay.[10]

The most effective way to jump-start essential reforms would be to end the concept of an entitlement program by requiring Congress to vote on every dollar spent, every year. As it stands now, programs are on automatic pilot, voted on by people who are no longer in power.[11] Congress votes a program into law, and spending continues indefinitely into the future. Authorizing every dollar spent every year would make the budgeting process larger and more complicated, but it would restore accountability and force lawmakers to make the tough choices they have been avoiding.

For Social Security, the retirement age at which people can begin collecting benefits should be gradually raised. With people living longer, it no longer makes sense to provide full retirement at age 67 for those born after 1960. Raising the retirement age would also take away federal disincentives that discourage people from working longer. More work benefits the economy, leading to economic growth. Additionally, Social Security benefit increases should be pegged to the price level in the economy rather than wage level. What a person needs to live, not what other people make, should determine Social Security payouts.

As part of a broader reform, the government should allow people to contribute a portion of their Social Security payments to a private account that they can pass on to their heirs. Private accounts can earn a much better rate of return than the current Social Security system, and they would also give people more control over their retirement savings. For those concerned about income inequality, this solution would also allow more people of average income to take advantage of the booming stock market returns that have mostly benefited those with assets in equities.

For Medicare, Washington should inject more competition into the system by allowing people to choose from a wide variety of plans. Medicare funds could be used to make these private plans affordable to seniors through premium supports that vary with income. Government policy shouldn't penalize people for staying on their private insurance rather than joining Medicare.

Regarding the Affordable Care Act, Washington should reform it, starting with modified community rating, which prevents insurance companies from charging older people more than three times as much as younger ones, and the employer-mandate penalty. While Washington's effort to extend coverage to the uninsured is admirable, requiring employers to provide the insurance or pay a fine is not an integral component of the ACA. The employer mandate has major unintended consequences, including discouraging hiring, which disproportionately affects new entrants to the workforce.

American health-care policy should harness the power of competition by repealing burdensome laws such as the ban on buying insurance across state lines and the preferential tax treatment given to employer-sponsored health plans. Additionally, funds previously appropriated to subsidize the ACA's health-care exchange and Medicaid expansion should be used to finance vouchers for the uninsured so they can purchase insurance on the private market. Insurers should be able to offer a broad array of plans, including inexpensive catastrophic health insurance, not just comprehensive, costly plans. If the goal of health-care reform is to provide insurance to more people, there are far less costly options than the ACA available.

At the state level, pensions for public-sector employees threaten to bankrupt state budgets. State governments should turn these pensions from defined-benefit plans, which promise a certain amount, to defined-contribution plans, where employees can choose how much of their salary they wish to invest, an amount usually matched by employers. Such a change would lessen the responsibility of younger workers and taxpayers to fund public-sector pensions, because pension costs would be paid at the present, not deferred to future generations. Defined-contribution plans have the added benefit of giving workers more control over their personal finances.

Perhaps more progress has been made in primary education reform than in the other topics discussed. Still, we need more young, enthusiastic teachers such as Kimberly Tett, whose story we told in Chapter 3, if American education is to improve rather than stagnate. Her experience at an innovative charter school in Chicago's South Side shows that talented teachers require environments that welcome their innovations. We will never know how many talented teachers left the profession due to discouragement.

Cities such as Washington and New York are using charter schools to improve educational outcomes and better prepare young people for the workforce. States including Louisiana and Arizona have added their own innovations to the mix, such as educational vouchers and education savings accounts. State and local governments should continue to carve out a greater role for charter schools and other education innovations. Most important, we should make sure that schools and teachers once again have the freedom to figure out what works based on their unique circumstances and talents.

After primary and secondary school, young Americans should recognize that attending a four-year college is not for everyone. More young people should consider community college and vocational training to prepare them for the workforce or for further study, and our culture should start giving these alternative options the respect they deserve. Matt Varzino's story in Chapter 4 shows the financial, professional, and educational benefits of attending community college, and successes similar to his are common.

At the federal level, the government should reform its costly student loan program, which increases the price of tuition and burdens students with mountains of debt that many will be unable to repay. The heavy burdens of student loan debt leave young Americans such as Annie Johnson, whom we interviewed in Chapter 4, feeling pressure to delay life milestones and further education. Student loan reforms would hold down the soaring costs of college and make way for stronger private-sector credit offerings that would provide loans based on an individual's ability to repay them. Young people should take the advice that Connor Wolf gave in Chapter 4: Treat decisions about college as investments.

Little justification exists for most occupational licensing laws. Except in fields where public safety is a legitimate concern (such as medicine), states should work to quickly abolish occupational licensing. We should not force people such as Becky Maples, who was once an aspiring cosmetologist, to work in a factory, as described in Chapter 5. Her dreams fell out of reach owing to occupational licensing laws that do little more than protect entrenched businesses from new competition.

Unlicensed florists, hair braiders, and interior designers hardly pose a danger to the public, but the availability of these jobs can make a world of difference to millennials, particularly those from underprivileged backgrounds. After Melony Armstrong overcame Mississippi's Board of Cosmetology, also described in Chapter 5, she was able to use hair braiding not only to improve her own life but also to provide opportunities for young people who wish to learn a valuable skill. Her victory set off a cycle of entrepreneurship that has shown what young Americans can do if left to themselves.

Labor-market regulations at both the federal and state level keep young people out of work. Minimum wages and mandates restricting unpaid internships deprive millennials of the experience they need for future employment success. At the federal level, the minimum wage should be frozen, if not eliminated. This would allow business owners such as Robert Davis, in Chapter 6, and Linda Mack, in the Introduction, to continue employing and training young people who have few professional skills but future potential.

Rather than restricting unpaid internships in the private sector, the government should ensure that this form of work, which is often more important to prospective employers than choice of major, is expanded so that young people can take full advantage of it. Recall that Katya Margolin, described in Chapter 6, told us that one of her unpaid internships ranked among her most fulfilling work.

America's problems have solutions. What we need is a joint effort on the part of young and old to force politicians to discuss the issues and begin implementing solutions. August Meyer and Claire and Sonny

Sommers do not want to pass a future of higher taxes on to their grand-children and great-grandchildren. They want solutions as much as anyone.

CHAPTER 8

·

CONCLUSION

Tens of millions of Americans are between the ages of 18 and 30. These disinherited Americans are, or soon will be, entering the workforce. Their situation is substantially worse than that of prior generations of Americans. It is not because they are less intelligent. It is not because they have worked less. It is not because they are any less deserving of the American dream. It is because Washington consciously made decisions that render their lives more difficult than those of their parents or grandparents. And their younger siblings, and their children, who are not yet 18, will be even worse off, all because Washington has refused to fix the problem.

In this book, we have heard the stories of several members of this disinherited generation. Their stories are not unique. We have interviewed and heard from many other members of this generation. It is impossible to hear these stories and not understand that members of this generation are now and—absent reforms—will continue to be worse off than their parents.

Their stories, and the related economic data underlying them, are an indictment of America's treatment of its young. A nation that prides itself on its future has mortgaged it. A nation that historically took pride in its youth culture has become a nation that steals from its young. People who should have fulfilling, productive lives are sidelined, unemployed, or underemployed. Meanwhile, America expects millennials and others of the disinherited generation to pay higher taxes so that middle-aged and elderly Americans, many of whom have better jobs and more assets, can receive more from Uncle Sam.

Jean Thompson, described in Chapter 1, has an undergraduate degree, four years of work experience, and a master's degree in public policy. Since graduating in 2012, she still cannot find work, despite multiple interviews. Something is very wrong with this picture. This is a problem that Jean's parents, both economists, did not face.

Mary Parrilli, in the Introduction, and Geoffrey Levesque, in Chapter 1, both in their twenties, have little faith they will receive back the money they are paying into Social Security. While they both believe people should take care of the elderly, and they understand that current retirees paid into the program while they worked, they do not see Social Security today as a fair deal. They are being made to bear the burden of unfunded promises while missing out on promised benefits. This is a problem that the parents and grandparents of Mary and Geoff did not face.

Tommy Groves, whose story we told in Chapter 2, was completely satisfied with his health-insurance policy, but it was cancelled because it did not meet the Affordable Care Act guidelines. He spent countless hours online and on the phone trying to enroll in the Washington, D.C., health exchange. Just before the deadline of March 31, 2014, he waited in line for hours to enroll in person. He was forced to buy a more expensive plan with a higher deductible that provided him no additional value. This is a problem that Tommy's parents did not face.

These are just a few examples of Washington's betrayal of America's young. Washington treats the young with little respect yet expects them to pay higher taxes in the future to fund lavish programs that they will probably never see.

Take Social Security and Medicare. These two programs consume a combined $4 out of every $10 of federal spending, and the share is going nowhere but up. The programs pay generous benefits to America's seniors while leaving the disinherited generation with the bill. Yet Washington's politicians, Republicans and Democrats alike, are unwilling to change course.

With the passage of the Social Security Act in 1935, America began to put in place a social safety net to help those in need. Since then, this social safety net has steadily mushroomed into a vast array of overlapping entitlement programs. New programs, such as the Affordable Care Act, which disproportionately benefit middle-aged and older Americans, are being added. The cost of these programs is borne by America's young people without their consent.

The disinherited generation has no powerful interest group to defend it. No lobby exists for getting rid of occupational licensing, and efforts to reform entitlement programs have gained only limited traction in Washington. Many government programs disburse concentrated benefits but have diffused costs, and the young consistently end up bearing the costs but missing out on the benefits. To the political powers that be, young people and their burdens are effectively invisible.

"Through a long sequence of accommodations to immediate contingencies and opportunities, we have built a system in which the electorate expects, and political officials provide, a higher level of personal benefits than of tax collections to pay for the benefits," notes Hudson Institute senior fellow Christopher DeMuth. "The difference is taxed to younger and future generations—to be paid in the future, by unknown subsets of them, through higher outright taxes, reduced benefits, debt defaults, or inflation. The situation is intractable because most of those being burdened are not voters (most are not even alive) and cannot be part of a constituency for reform."[1]

Unfortunately, even if young people ignore the political process, the political process does not ignore them. Greater engagement by the young alone will not sufficiently pressure Washington to change course. Americans of all age groups need to understand the level of unfairness current policy creates. At the same time, Washington must allow young people to use the skills they have. This means America must evaluate its countless regulations, laws, and policies through the prism of how they affect new entrants to the workforce. Some regulations need to be abandoned in favor of a more hands-off approach that will let young people flourish.

The Internet and technology fields are currently the most unregulated sector of the economy. In this arena, America's youth are in high demand and add significant value to the creation, production, and distribution processes. Our young people are as talented and as deserving of success as their parents and grandparents. Rather than hindering their progress, we need to provide the right conditions for them to succeed.

Youth unemployment is a serious matter, and not only for the young. A society that cannot offer millennials work will see the brightest flee to places that have more opportunities. Others, less entrepreneurial, will stay and struggle to succeed in a country that frustrates their interests. Still others will give up on their future and instead try to collect government benefits. Hard-won college degrees will atrophy. The vaunted American work ethic admired by Alexis de Tocqueville will slowly disappear. Youth unemployment leads to low self-esteem that can last a lifetime. It delays life milestones, such as the first car, the first apartment, marriage, or the birth of children. Some young people resort to crime, either out of boredom or as a way to make ends meet.

A country that betrays its youth cannot fully prosper. This book has tried to give a voice to a disinherited generation of scarred young Americans at risk of being lost—and if they go missing, they will take with them the future of America. Throughout this book we have related stories of well-intentioned programs, laws, and regulations that went awry and morphed into behemoths unimaginable to their initial supporters.

The future of America can be saved, but only if our government ceases its betrayal of youth. Whatever the government hopes to win in devising policies that leave an entire generation under assault, its victory is Pyrrhic, with only young victims in its wake. We must restore the birthright of the millennials and other young people, and the time to do so is now.

ACKNOWLEDGMENTS

First and foremost, we are indebted to all the young people who have shared their life stories with us. These stories form the core of the book. Jason Church, Julie Laslo, Geoffrey Levesque, Michael Lopato, Becky Maples, Katya Margolin, Mary Parrilli, Kimberly Tett, Matt Varzino, and Connor Wolf all told us about their lives and are featured under their real names. Others, such as Stacy Bell, Robert Davis, James Findley, Tommy Groves, Annie Johnson, Sammy Page, and Jean Thompson, spoke to us and are featured under pseudonyms. You know who you are, we know who you are, and we thank you.

We are grateful to the non-millennials we spoke with about their experiences, including Melony Armstrong, owner of Naturally Speaking Salons; Oscar Cardoza, a maintenance worker in South Carolina; Rebecca Friedrichs, a veteran teacher in Orange County, California; Linda Mack, owner of Silver Cycles in suburban Maryland; August Meyer, of Roseville, Minnesota; Narendra Sharma, an educator of low-income children in South Carolina; and Claire and Sonny Sommers, from Brooklyn.

We would like to thank the Economics21 research staff—Claire Monteiro, Jason Russell, and Matthew Sabas—for their assistance and enthusiasm, as well as interns Preston Cooper, Steven Gordon, Patrick Holland, Nehmat Kaur, Gloria Kim, Tom Pacer, Yohan Sumathipala, and Amanda Swysgood.

We are grateful to the entire Encounter Books team, Roger Kimball, Lauren Miklos, Heather Ohle, Sam Schneider, and Katherine Wong. Our editor, Molly Powell, paid attention to every comma and hyphen, and rapidly and accurately turned around numerous drafts. We also owe thanks to Robert Asahina for additional editing input.

We benefited, as we always do, from the support and critical comments of our Manhattan Institute colleagues: Judah Bellin, Stephen Eide,

Sarah Ferrara, Yevgeniy Feyman, Leigh Harrington, Howard Husock, Michele Jacob, Katherine Lazarski, Vanessa Mendoza, Larry Mone, Natalie Nakamura, Bernadette Serton, Robert Sherwood, and Scott Winship. Clark Neily, of the Institute for Justice, also provided us with insightful comments on occupational licensing.

Our deepest gratitude goes to Frederick Sommers, emeritus professor of philosophy at Brandeis University. Professor Sommers commented on initial drafts and wrote: "You have all the economic facts. . . . Big government dooms the young to be ineffectual and dependent on the parents and the government. There is no reply." We appreciate all the wisdom we received from Professor Sommers, who died on October 2, 2014, at the age of 91.

No book is written in a vacuum, and this one is no exception. We would like to thank our parents, Julie and Tom Meyer, and Gabriel and Ellen Roth, for all their support. The influence of philosophy professors Douglas Rasmussen and Paul Gaffney led us to see *Disinherited* as more than an economic-policy book—perpetuating policies that place young people at a disadvantage has deep moral implications. Harold Furchtgott-Roth offered invaluable comments, and the children—Leon, Deborah, Jeremy, Chani, Francesca, Godfrey, Theodore, and Richard Furchtgott—provided motivation and inspiration.

ENDNOTES

Introduction and Summary: The Overarching Problem

1 "Current Population Survey," Bureau of Labor Statistics, January 2015.

2 Ibid.

3 Ibid.

4 Richard Fry, "A Rising Share of Young Adults Live in Their Parents' Home," Pew Research Center, August 1, 2013, http://www.pewsocialtrends .org/2013/08/01/a-rising-share-of-young-adults-live-in-their-parents-home/.

5 Robert J. Samuelson, "The (Millennial) Parent Trap," *Washington Post*, August 3, 2014, http://www.washingtonpost.com/opinions/robert-samuelson-the-millennial-parent-trap /2014/08/03/224ddb78-199c-11e4-85b6-c1451e622637_story.html.

6 "America's Young Adults at 27: Labor Market Activity, Education, and Household Composition: Results from a Longitudinal Survey," Bureau of Labor Statistics, March 26, 2014, http://www.bls.gov/news.release/pdf/nlsyth.pdf.

7 "The Daily History of the Debt Results," U.S. Department of the Treasury, TreasuryDirect, January 12, 2015, http://www.treasurydirect.gov/NP/debt/search?startMonth=08&startDay =06&startYear=2014&endMonth=&endDay=&endYear=.

8 Joe Luppino-Esposito, "State Budget Solutions' 2014 Unfunded Pension Liabilities Report," State Budget Solutions, November 12, 2014, https://docs.google.com/spreadsheets /d/1uaNVzfeKQ3XD_M696zuuzIWafHnaslkJfmeRODi137I/edit#gid=0.

9 Eugene Steuerle, "Why Delayed Social Security Reform Costs Us," *The Government We Deserve* (blog), July 29, 2014, http://blog.governmentwedeserve.org/2014/07/29 /why-delayed-social-security-reform-costs-us/.

10 "Summary of Receipts, Outlays, and Surpluses or Deficits," Office of Management and Budget, accessed November 29, 2014, http://www.whitehouse.gov/omb/budget/historicals.

11 "The Budget and Economic Outlook: 2014 to 2024," Congressional Budget Office, February 2014, http://www.cbo.gov/sites/default/files/cbofiles/attachments/45010-Outlook2014_Feb .pdf.

12 Dale H. Yamamoto, "Health Care Costs—From Birth to Death," Society of Actuaries, June 2013, http://www.healthcostinstitute.org/files/Age-Curve-Study_0.pdf.

13 Matthew Reed and Debbie Cochrane, "Student Debt and the Class of 2012," Institute for College Access & Success, December 2013, http://projectonstudentdebt.org/files/pub /classof2012.pdf.

14 Dick M. Carpenter II et al., "License to Work: A National Study of Burdens from Occupational Licensing," Institute for Justice, May 2012, pp. 12–13, https://www.ij.org/ images/pdf_folder/economic_liberty/occupational_licensing /licensetowork.pdf.

15 "Wage and salary workers paid hourly rates with earnings at or below the prevailing Federal minimum wage by selected characteristics," Bureau of Labor Statistics, 2014, http:// www.bls.gov/cps/cpsaat44.pdf.

16 "Unemployment Rate by Age Group," Eurostat 2013, http://epp.eurostat.ec.europa.eu/tgm/table.do?tab=table&init=1&plugin=1&language=en&pcode=tsdec460.

Chapter 1: Unfunded Promises

1 "The Daily History of the Debt Results," TreasuryDirect, accessed January 12, 2015, http://www.treasurydirect.gov/NP/debt/search?startMonth=08&startDay=06&startYear=2014&endMonth=&endDay=&endYear=.

2 "The 2014 Long-Term Projections for Social Security: Additional Information," Congressional Budget Office, December 2014, http://www.cbo.gov/sites/default/files/cbofiles/attachments/49795-Social_Security_Update.pdf.

3 Laurence Kotlikoff, "Assessing Fiscal Sustainability," Mercatus Center, December 12, 2013, http://mercatus.org/publication/assessing-fiscal-sustainability.

4 Luppino-Esposito, "State Budget Solutions' 2014 Unfunded Liabilities Report."

5 Christopher DeMuth, "Our Democratic Debt," *National Review*, July 21, 2014, http://www.nationalreview.com/article/392771/our-democratic-debt-chris-demuth.

6 Laurence Kotlikoff, "Assessing Fiscal Sustainability," Mercatus Center, December 12, 2013, http://mercatus.org/publication/assessing-fiscal-sustainability.

7 Don Watkins, *RooseveltCare: How Social Security Is Sabotaging the Land of Self-Reliance* (Irvine, Calif.: Ayn Rand Institute Press, 2014), p. 114.

8 "An Update to the Budget and Economic Outlook: 2014 to 2024," Congressional Budget Office, August 2014, http://www.cbo.gov/sites/default/files/cbofiles/attachments/45653-OutlookUpdate_2014_Aug.pdf.

9 "The 2014 Long-Term Budget Outlook," Congressional Budget Office, July 15, 2014, http://www.cbo.gov/publication/45471.

10 Eugene Steuerle, *Dead Men Ruling: How to Restore Fiscal Freedom and Rescue Our Future* (New York: Century Foundation, 2014).

11 "Status of the Social Security and Medicare Programs," Social Security and Medicare Boards of Trustees, Social Security Administration, 2014, http://www.ssa.gov/oact/trsum/.

12 "2014 Annual Report," Boards of Trustees, Federal Hospital Insurance, and Federal Supplementary Medical Insurance Trust Funds, July 28, 2014, http://www.cms.gov/Research-Statistics-Data-and-Systems/Statistics-Trends-and-Reports/ReportsTrustFunds/Downloads/TR2014.pdf.

13 "The 2014 Long-Term Budget Outlook," Congressional Budget Office, July 15, 2014, p. 10, http://www.cbo.gov/publication/45471.

14 "Topic 751—Social Security and Medicare Withholding Rates," Internal Revenue Service, July 16, 2014, http://www.irs.gov/taxtopics/tc751.html.

15 Nicholas Kristof, "The Wrong Side of History," *New York Times*, November 18, 2009.

16 Ibid.

17 Robin Toner, "New Deal Debate for a New Era," *New York Times*, August 1, 2007.

18 Larry Dewitt, "The Development of Social Security in America," *Social Security Bulletin* 70, no. 3 (2010), http://www.ssa.gov/policy/docs/ssb/v70n3/v70n3p1.html.

19 "Updated Budget Projections: 2014 to 2024," Congressional Budget Office, April 14, 2014, p. 3, http://www.cbo.gov/publication/45229.

20 "Social Security Beneficiary Statistics: Number of Beneficiaries Receiving Benefits on December 31, 1970–2013," Social Security Administration, http://www.ssa.gov/oact/STATS/OASDIbenies.html.

21 "Updated Budget Projections: 2014 to 2024," Congressional Budget Office, April 14, 2014, http://www.cbo.gov/publication/45229.

22 "2014 Annual Report," Board of Trustees, Federal Old-Age and Survivors Insurance and Federal Disability Insurance Trust Funds, July 28, 2014, p. 191, http://www.ssa.gov/oact /tr/2014/tr2014.pdf.

23 "The 2014 Long-Term Budget Outlook," Congressional Budget Office, July 15, 2014, http:// www.cbo.gov/publication/45471.

24 "History of SSA During the Johnson Administration 1963–1968," Social Security Administration, http://www.ssa.gov/history/ssa/lbjhistory.html.

25 "2011 Medicare & Medicaid Statistical Supplement," Centers for Medicare and Medicaid Services, Table 3.1.

26 "The Facts on Medicare Spending and Financing," The Henry J. Kaiser Family Foundation, July 28, 2014, http://kff.org/medicare/fact-sheet/medicare-spending-and-financing-fact-sheet/.

27 "2002 Annual Report," Boards of Trustees, Federal Hospital Insurance and Federal Supplementary Medical Insurance Trust Funds, March 26, 2002.

28 "Medicare Enrollment: National Trends 1966–2008," Centers for Medicare and Medicaid Services.

29 "2014 Annual Report," Boards of Trustees, Federal Hospital Insurance and Federal Supplementary Medical Insurance Trust Funds, July 28, 2014.

30 Ibid.

31 Ibid.

32 Ibid.

33 "OASDI and HI Annual Income Rates, Cost Rates, and Balances, Calendar Years 2014–90," Table V1.G2, p. 198 in "2014 Annual Report," Board of Trustees, Federal Old-Age and Survivors Insurance and Federal Disability Insurance Trust Funds," July 28, 2014, http:// www.ssa.gov/oact/tr/2014/tr2014.pdf.

34 "Topic 751—Social Security and Medicare Withholding Rates," Internal Revenue Service, July 16, 2014, http://www.irs.gov/taxtopics/tc751.html.

35 "Social Security Programs Throughout the World: Europe, 2010," Social Security Administration Office of Retirement and Disability Policy, SSA Publication No. 13-11801, August 2010, http://www.ssa.gov/policy/docs/progdesc/ssptw/2010-2011/europe /ssptw10europe.pdf.

36 Luppino-Esposito, "State Budget Solutions' 2014 Unfunded Pension Liabilities Report."

37 "Budget Processes in the States," National Association of State Budget Officers, Summer 2008, http://www.nasbo.org/sites/default/files/BP_2008.pdf.

38 "The Widening Gap Update," Pew Center on the States, June 2012, http://www.pewtrusts. org/~/media/legacy/uploadedfiles/pcs_assets/2012/PewPensionsUpdatepdf.pdf.

39 "GASB Pension Revamp Introduces Major Improvements," Governmental Accounting Standards Board, Summer 2012, http://www.gasb.org/cs/ContentServer?site=GASB&c= GASBContent_C&pagename=GASB/GASBContent_C/UsersArticlePage&cid= 1176160319691.

40 Andrew G. Biggs and Kent A. Smetters, "Understanding the Argument for Market Valuation of Public Pension Liabilities," American Enterprise Institute, May 2013, http:// www.aei.org/files/2013/05/29/-understanding-the-argument-for-market-valuation-of-public-pension-liabilities_10491782445.pdf.

41 "Union Members—2014," Bureau of Labor Statistics, January 23, 2015, http://www.bls.gov /news.release/pdf/union2.pdf.

42 Unpublished calculations from William McBride, Tax Foundation.

43 "Fiscal Confidence Index: July 2014 Results," Peter G. Peterson Foundation, July 29, 2014, http://pgpf.org/_fiscalconfidenceindex/results-2014July.

Chapter 2: Paying for Parents' Health Care

1 Dale H. Yamamoto, "Health Care Costs—From Birth to Death," Society of Actuaries, June 2013, http://www.healthcostinstitute.org/files/Age-Curve-Study_0.pdf.

2 Ezra Klein and Sarah Kliff, "Obama's Last Campaign: Inside the White House Plan to Sell Obamacare," *Washington Post*, July 17, 2013.

3 Mark Hemingway, "Selling Obamacare," *Reason*, August/September 2014, http://reason .com/archives/2014/07/01/selling-obamacare/.

4 Ibid.

5 "Health Insurance Marketplace: Summary Enrollment Report for the Initial Annual Open Enrollment Period," Department of Health and Human Services, May 1, 2014, http://aspe .hhs.gov/health/reports/2014/MarketPlaceEnrollment/Apr2014/ib_2014apr_enrollment .pdf.

6 "Consumer Expenditure Survey, Table 4500," Bureau of Labor Statistics, September 2014, http://www.bls.gov/cex/2013/combined/sage.pdf.

7 "The Obamacare Impact: How the Health Law Affects the Affordability of Your Health Care," Manhattan Institute for Policy Research, June 2014, unpublished data, http://www .manhattan-institute.org/knowyourrates/.

8 Ibid.

9 "Patient Protection and Affordable Care Act: Effect on Long-Term Federal Budget Outlook Largely Depends on Whether Cost Containment Sustained," United States Government Accountability Office, January 2013, http://www.gao.gov/assets/660/651702 .pdf.

10 "The Looming Premium Rate Shock," U.S. House of Representatives Committee on Energy and Commerce, May 13, 2013, http://energycommerce.house.gov/sites/republicans .energycommerce.house.gov/files/analysis/insurancepremiums/FinalReport.pdf.

11 "Health Insurance Marketplace: Summary Enrollment Report for the Initial Annual Open Enrollment Period," Department of Health and Human Services, May 1, 2014.

12 "Essential Health Benefits," HealthCare.gov, accessed August 5, 2014, https:// www.healthcare.gov/glossary/essential-health-benefits/.

13 "Percent Distribution of Households, by Selected Characteristics Within Income Quintile and Top 5 Percent in 2012," Table HINC-05 in "Annual Social and Economic Supplement 2013," U.S. Census Bureau, accessed August 5, 2014, https://www.census.gov/hhes/www /cpstables/032013/hhinc/toc.htm.

14 Edmund F. Haislmaier, "Testimony Before Committee on the Judiciary Subcommittee on Intellectual Property, United States House of Representatives," Heritage Foundation, May 18, 2012, http://www.heritage.org/research/testimony/2013/06/health-care-consolidation- and-competition-after-ppaca.

15 "Payments of Penalties for Being Uninsured Under the Affordable Care Act: 2014 Update," Congressional Budget Office, June 5, 2014, http://www.cbo.gov/publication/45397.

16 "The Fee You Pay If You Don't Have Health Coverage," HealthCare.gov, accessed August 5, 2014, https://www.healthcare.gov/what-if-i-dont-have-health-coverage/.

17 "The Obamacare Impact: How the Health Law Affects the Affordability of Your Health Care," Manhattan Institute for Policy Research, June 2014, unpublished data, http://www .manhattan-institute.org/knowyourrates/.

18 "Medical Expenditure Panel Survey," Agency for Healthcare Research & Quality, U.S. Department of Health and Human Resources, 2014.

19 Casey B. Mulligan, "The ACA: Some Unpleasant Welfare Arithmetic" (working paper no. 20020, National Bureau of Economic Research, March 2014), http://www.nber.org/papers /w20020.

20 Bill McInturff and Micah Roberts, "Presentation of Findings from National Research Conducted Among Business Decision-Makers: September–October 2013," Public Opinion

Strategies survey conducted on behalf of the International Franchise Association and the U.S. Chamber of Commerce, October 2013, http://pos.org/documents/ifa-chamber _survey_findings.pdf.

21 Ibid.

22 "Employed Persons by Class of Worker and Part-Time Status," Bureau of Labor Statistics, January 2015, http://www.bls.gov/news.release/empsit.to8.htm.

23 "Current Population Survey," Bureau of Labor Statistics, January 2015.

24 Linda J. Blumberg, John Holahan, and Matthew Buettgens, "Why Not Just Eliminate the Employer Mandate?" Urban Institute, May 2014, http://www.urban.org /UploadedPDF/413117-Why-Not-Just-Eliminate-the-Employer-Mandate.pdf.

25 Tom Gara, "Union Letter: Obamacare 'Will Destroy the Very Health and Well-Being' of Workers," *Corporate Intelligence* (blog), *Wall Street Journal*, July 12, 2013.

26 "Updated Estimates of the Effects of Insurance Coverage Provisions of the Affordable Care Act—CBO's April 2014 Baseline," Congressional Budget Office, April 14, 2014, http://www .cbo.gov/sites/default/files/cbofiles/attachments/43900-2014-04-ACAtables.pdf.

27 Tom Miller, "Employer Health Plan Sponsors: Running Harder, to Stay in Place," Economics21, Manhattan Institute, June 27, 2014, http://economics21.org/commentary /employer-health-plan-sponsors-running-harder-stay-place.

28 "Labor Market Effects of the Affordable Care Act: Updated Estimates," Congressional Budget Office, February 2014, http://www.cbo.gov/sites/default/files/cbofiles /attachments/45010-breakout-AppendixC.pdf

29 "Current Population Survey," Bureau of Labor Statistics, January 2015.

30 Ed Morrissey, "Pelosi: Hey, Quit Your Job—We'll Pay for Your Health Coverage!" *Hot Air,* May 15, 2010, http://hotair.com/archives/2010/05/15/pelosi-hey-quit-your-job-well-pay-for-your-health-coverage/.

31 Casey B. Mulligan, *Side Effects: The Economic Consequences of the Health Reform* (Flossmoor, IL: JMJ Economics, 2014).

32 "Updated Estimates of the Effects of Insurance Coverage Provisions of the Affordable Care Act—CBO's April 2014 Baseline," Congressional Budget Office, April 14, 2014, http://www .cbo.gov/sites/default/files/cbofiles/attachments/43900-2014-04-ACAtables.pdf.

33 "The 2014 Long-Term Budget Outlook," Congressional Budget Office, July 2014, https:// www.cbo.gov/sites/default/files/45471-Long-TermBudgetOutlook_7-29.pdf.

34 Charles Blahous, "The Affordable Care Act's Optional Medicaid Expansion: Considerations Facing State Governments," Mercatus Center, George Mason University, March 5, 2013, mercatus.org/publicationaffordable-care-acts-optional-medicaid-expansion-considerations-facing-state-governments.

35 Sarah L. Taubman et al., "Medicaid Increases Emergency-Department Use: Evidence from Oregon's Health Insurance Experiment," *Science* 17 (January 2014), pp. 263–268, http:// www.sciencemag.org/content/343/6168/263.abstract.

36 "Crisis Hit GP Surgeries Forced to Turn Away Millions of Patients," Royal College of General Practitioners, July 28, 2014, http://www.rcgp.org.uk/news/2014/july/crisis-hit-gp-surgeries-forced-to-turn-away-millions-of-patients.aspx.

37 "GME Funding: How to Fix the Doctor Shortage," Association of American Medical Colleges, accessed August 5, 2014, https://www.aamc.org/advocacy/campaigns_and _coalitions/fixdocshortage/.

Chapter 3: The Failure of Primary and Secondary Education

1 Terry M. Moe, *Special Interest: Teachers Unions and America's Public Schools* (Washington, D.C.: Brookings Institution, 2011), p. 266.

2 "PISA 2012 Results in Focus," Programme for International Student Assessment, OECD, 2014, http://www.oecd.org/pisa/keyfindings/pisa-2012-results-overview.pdf.

3 "Public High School Four-Year On-Time Graduation Rates and Event Dropout Rates: School Years 2010–11 and 2011–12," National Center for Education Statistics, U.S. Department of Education, 2014, http://nces.ed.gov/pubs2014/2014391.pdf.

4 "NAEP as an Indicator of Students' Academic Preparedness for College," The Nation's Report Card, U.S. Department of Education, 2014, http://www.nationsreportcard.gov /reading_math_g12_2013/#/preparedness.

5 "NAEP: District Profiles," National Center for Education Statistics, U.S. Department of Education, accessed July 18, 2014, http://nces.ed.gov/nationsreportcard/districts/.

6 "PISA 2012 Results in Focus," Programme for International Student Assessment, OECD, 2014, http://www.oecd.org/pisa/keyfindings/pisa-2012-results-overview.pdf.

7 Paul E. Peterson et al., "Are U.S. Students Ready to Compete?" *Education Next* 11, no. 4 (Fall 2011), http://educationnext.org/are-u-s-students-ready-to-compete/.

8 Jill Casner-Lotto, Elyse Rosenblum, and Mary Wright, "The Ill-Prepared U.S. Workforce: Exploring the Challenges of Employer-Provided Workforce Readiness Training," The Conference Board, 2009, http://www.shrm.org/Research/SurveyFindings/Articles /Documents/BED-09Workforce_RR.pdf.

9 Tom Loveless, "How Well are American Students Learning?" Brown Center on Education Policy, Brookings Institution, October 2006, http://www.brookings.edu/~/media/research /files/reports/2006/10/education%20loveless/10education_loveless.pdf.

10 "The Education Crisis: Statistics," Eli and Edythe Broad Foundation, accessed July 18, 2014, http://www.broadeducation.org/about/crisis_stats.html.

11 "Table 236.55. Total and Current Expenditures Per Pupil in Public Elementary and Secondary Schools: Selected Years, 1919–20 Through 2010–11," National Center for Education Statistics, U.S. Department of Education, accessed August 28, 2014, http://nces .ed.gov/programs/digest/d13/tables/dt13_236.55.asp.

12 "Improving Basic Programs Operated by Local Educational Agencies (Title I, Part A)," U.S. Department of Education, accessed July 18 2014, http://www2.ed.gov/programs/titleiparta /index.html.

13 Jay G. Chambers et al., "State and Local Implementation of the No Child Left Behind Act: Volume VI—Targeting and Uses of Federal Education Funds," U.S. Department of Education, 2009, http://www2.ed.gov/rschstat/eval/disadv/nclb-targeting/nclb-targeting .pdf.

14 "Table 92. Staff Employed in Public Elementary and Secondary School Systems, by Type of Assignment," National Center for Education Statistics, U.S. Department of Education, May 2012, http://nces.ed.gov/programs/digest/d12/tables/dt12_092.asp.

15 "Frequently Asked Questions," Office of Labor Relations, New York City Department of Education, 2007, http://schools.nyc.gov/NR/rdonlyres/7E50C743-72E1-4BDC-8F40- E8DDED86570A/0/LaborFAQs200742407.pdf.

16 Matthew Richmond, "The Hidden Half: School Employees Who Don't Teach," Thomas B. Fordham Institute, August 2014, http://edex.s3-us-west-2.amazonaws.com/publication /pdfs/Hidden-Half-School-Employees-Who-Dont-Teach-FINAL_0.pdf.

17 Benjamin Scafidi, "The School Staffing Surge: Decades of Employment Growth in America's Public Schools," Friedman Foundation for Educational Choice, October 2012, http://www.edchoice.org/CMSModules/EdChoice/FileLibrary/931/The-School-Staffing- Surge--Decades-of-Employment-Growth-in-Americas-Public-Schools.pdf.

18 "Table 90. Estimated Average Annual Salary of Teachers in Public Elementary and Secondary Schools: Selected Years, 1959–60 through 2011–12," National Center for Education Statistics, U.S. Department of Education, 2012, http://nces.ed.gov /programs/digest/d12/tables/dt12_090.asp?referrer=report.

19 "Teacher Trends," National Center for Education Statistics, U.S. Department of Education, accessed July 18 2014, http://nces.ed.gov/fastfacts/display.asp?id=28.

20 Raj Chetty, John N. Friedman, and Jonah E. Rockoff, "Measuring the Impacts of Teachers II: Teacher Value-Added and Student Outcomes in Adulthood," *American Economic Review* 104, no. 9 (September 2014), http://obs.rc.fas.harvard.edu/chetty/w19424.pdf. These numbers are discounted at a 5 percent annual rate.

21 Byron Auguste, Paul Kihn, and Matt Miller, "Closing the Talent Gap: Attracting and Retaining Top-Third Graduates to Careers in Teaching," Mckinsey and Company, September 2010, http://mckinseyonsociety.com/downloads/reports/Education/Closing _the_talent_gap.pdf.

22 Eric A. Hanushek, Marc Piopiunik, and Simon Wiederhold, "The Value of Smarter Teachers: International Evidence on Teacher Cognitive Skills and Student Performance" (working paper no. 20727, National Bureau of Economic Reseaerch, December 2014), http://papers.nber.org/tmp/66670-w20727.pdf.

23 "Protecting Bad Teachers: Tenure," Teachers Union Exposed, Center for Union Facts, accessed July 18 2014, http://www.teachersunionexposed.com/protecting.cfm.

24 Jason Felch, Jessica Garrison, and Jason Song, "Bar Set Low for Lifetime Job in L.A. Schools," *Los Angeles Times,* December 20, 2009.

25 "Protecting Bad Teachers: Tenure," Teachers Union Exposed, Center for Union Facts, accessed July 18, 2014.

26 Scott Waldman, "Solving Puzzle of Bad Teachers," *Times-Union (Albany)*, October 24, 2011.

27 Luppino-Esposito, "State Budget Solutions' 2014 Unfunded Liabilities Report."

28 "Open Secrets: Teachers Unions," Center for Responsive Politics, accessed December 8, 2014, https://www.opensecrets.org/industries/indus.php?ind=L1300.

29 Moe, *Special Interest,* p. 8.

30 Editorial, "Witness Protection for Teachers," *Wall Street Journal*, November 24, 2003.

31 Rolf M. Treu, *Vergara v. California*, Superior Court of the State of California, June 10, 2014, http://apps.washingtonpost.com/g/documents/local/court-decision-in-vergara-v -california/1031/.

32 "IMPACTplus for Teachers," District of Columbia Public Schools, http://dcps.dc.gov /DCPS/Files/downloads/In-the-Classroom/Ensuring-Teacher-Success/2013-2014%20 IMPACTplus%20For%20Teachers.pdf.

33 Thomas Dee and James Wyckoff, "Incentives, Selection, and Teacher Performance: Evidence from IMPACT" (working paper no. 19529, National Bureau of Economic Research, October 2013). http://www.nber.org/papers/w19529

34 "2013 Adjusted Cohort 4 Year Graduation Rates," State of New Jersey Department of Education, http://www.state.nj.us/education/data/grate/2013/.

35 "Newark Public Schools Celebrates Its Most Effective Teachers with $1.3 Million in Merit Bonuses," Newark Public Schools, August 23, 2013, http://www.nps.k12.nj.us/press-releases /newark-public-schools-celebrates-effective-teachers-1-3-million-merit-bonuses/.

36 "New York City Charter Schools: 2014–2015 Enrollment Lottery Estimates," New York City Charter School Center, April 2014, http://www.nyccharterschools.org/sites/default/files /resources/Lottery2014FinalReport.pdf.

37 "Students Names on Charter School Waiting Lists Top One Millon for the First Time," National Alliance for Public Charter Schools, May 5, 2014, http://www.publiccharters.org /press/waiting-list-2014/.

38 William G. Howell, Martin R. West, and Paul E. Peterson, "Reform Agenda Gains Strength," *Education Next* 13, no. 1 (Winter 2013), http://educationnext.org /reform-agenda-gains-strength/.

39 Caroline M. Hoxby, Sonali Murarka, and Jenny Kang, "How New York City's Charter Schools Affect Achievement, August 2009 Report," chap. 4, p. 1 in *New York City Charter*

Schools Evaluation Project, September 2009, http://users.nber.org/~schools
/charterschooleval/how_NYC_charter_schools_affect_achievement_sept2009.pdf.

40 Ibid., p. 11.

41 Meagan Batdorff et al., "Charter School Funding: Inequity Expands," School Choice
Demonstration Project, University of Arkansas, 2014, http://www.uaedreform.org
/wp-content/uploads/charter-funding-inequity-expands.pdf.

42 Hoxby, Murarka, and Kang, "How New York City's Charter Schools Affect Achivement,
August 2009 Report," chap. 5, p. 3.

43 Jason L. Riley, *Please Stop Helping Us: How Liberals Make It Harder for Blacks to Succeed*
(New York: Encounter Books, 2014), pp. 123–124.

44 "Highlights of 2014 State Exam Results," Success Academy Charter Schools, http://
successacademies.org/site/uploads/2014/08/SA_StateTestResults2014_081514.pdf.

45 Marcus Winters, "The Effect of Co-locations on Student Achievement in NYC Public
Schools," Center for State and Local Leadership at the Manhattan Institute, February 2014,
http://www.manhattan-institute.org/pdf/cr_85.pdf.

46 "2012 School Report Cards," Louisiana Department of Education, 2013, http://
www.louisianabelieves.com/data/reportcards/2013/.

47 "Parents Applaud DOJ Retreat on Opposition to Louisiana Educational Choice Program,"
Louisiana Federation for Children, November 19, 2013, http://louisiana4children.org
/news-releases/parents-applaud-doj-retreat-on-opposition-to-louisiana-educational-
choice-program.

48 "Louisiana Scholarship Program: Parental Satisfaction Survey Results," Louisiana
Federation for Children and Louisiana Black Alliance for Educational Options, April 2014,
http://s3.amazonaws.com/LouisianaFederationforChildren/uploads/202/original
/2014_Parental_Satisfaction_Survey.pdf?1398185286.

49 *Oless Brumfiel, et al. and United States of America v. William J. Dodd Superintendent of
Public Education, et al., United States' Memorandum in Support of Its Motion for Further
Relief,* August 22, 2013, http://media.nola.com/education_impact/other/US%20DOJ%20
petition%20vouchers%20deseg.pdf.

50 Christine H. Rossell, "A Report on the Effect of the 2012–13 Scholarship Program on
Racial Imbalance in Louisiana School Districts Under a Desegregation Court Order as of
2012–13," report prepared in the case of *Brumfield v. Dodd*, November 7, 2013, http://images
.politico.com/global/2013/11/07/lavoucheraff2.html.

51 Jonathan Butcher and Jason Bedrick, "Schooling Satisfaction: Arizona Parents' Opinions
on Using Education Savings Accounts," Friedman Foundation for Educational Choice,
October 2013, http://www.edchoice.org/CMSModules/EdChoice/FileLibrary/1019
/SCHOOLING-SATISFACTION-Arizona-Parents-Opinions-on-Using-Education-
Savings-Accounts.pdf.

52 "Private Schools: Who Benefits?" Programme for International Student Assessment,
OECD, 2011, http://www.oecd.org/pisa/pisaproducts/pisainfocus/48482894.pdf.

53 Andrew J. Coulson, "Comparing Public, Private, and Market Schools: The International
Evidence," *Journal of School Choice* 3 (2009), pp. 31–54, http://object.cato.org/sites/cato.org
/files/articles/10.1.1.175.6495.pdf

54 Eric Bettinger, "Educational Vouchers in International Contexts," *Handbook of the
Economics of Education* 4 (2011), pp. 551–570.

55 Martin West and Ludger Woessman, "School Choice International: Higher Private School
Share Boosts National Test Scores," *Education Next* 9, no. 1 (Winter 2009).

56 Paul E. Peterson, "Charter Schools and Student Performance," *Wall Street Journal*, March
16, 2010.

57 James P. Kelly and Benjamin Scafidi, "More Than Scores: An Analysis of Why and How
Parents Choose Private Schools," Friedman Foundation for Educational Choice, November

2013, http://www.edchoice.org/CMSModules/EdChoice/FileLibrary/1031/More-Than-Scores.pdf.

58 Patrick J. Wolf and Michael McShane, "Is the Juice Worth the Squeeze? A Benefit/Cost Analysis of the District of Columbia Opportunity Scholarship Program," *Education Finance and Policy* 8, no. 1 (Winter 2013), pp. 74–99.

Chapter 4: Drowning in College Debt

1   "About Berea College: History," Berea College, accessed August 8, 2014, http://www.berea.edu/about/history/.

2   "Top-Performing Endowments," *Pensions & Investments,* February 3, 2014, http://www.pionline.com/article/20140203/INTERACTIVE/140139989/top-performing-endowments.

3   "About Berea College: Quick Facts," Berea College, accessed August 8, 2014, http://www.berea.edu/about/quick-facts/.

4   Blake Ellis, "Average Student Loan Debt: $29,400," CNN Money, December 5, 2013, http://money.cnn.com/2013/12/04/pf/college/student-loan-debt/.

5   "Unemployment Rates by Age, Sex, and Marital Status, Seasonally Adjusted," Bureau of Labor Statistics, January 2015, http://www.bls.gov/web/empsit/cpseea10.htm.

6   Heidi Shierholz, Alyssa Davis, and Will Kimball, "The Class of 2014," Economic Policy Institute, May 1, 2014, http://www.epi.org/publication/class-of-2014/.

7   Jaison R. Abel, Richard Deitz, and Yaqin Su, "Are Recent College Graduates Finding Good Jobs?" *Current Issues in Economics and Finance, Federal Reserve Bank of New York* 20, no. 1 (2014), http://www.newyorkfed.org/research/current_issues/ci20-1.pdf.

8   Ibid.

9   "Trends in Student Aid 2014," College Board, https://secure-media.collegeboard.org/digitalServices/misc/trends/2014-trends-student-aid-report-final.pdf.

10 "Default Rates Continue to Rise for Federal Student Loans," U.S. Department of Education, September 30, 2013, http://www.ed.gov/news/press-releases/default-rates-continue-rise-federal-student-loans.

11 "Quarterly Report on Household Debt and Credit," Federal Reserve Bank of New York, November 2014, http://www.newyorkfed.org/householdcredit/2014-q3/data/pdf/HHDC_2014Q3.pdf.

12 Donghoon Lee, "Household Debt and Credit: Student Debt," Federal Reserve Bank of New York, February 28, 2013, http://www.newyorkfed.org/newsevents/mediaadvisory/2013/Lee022813.pdf.

13 "Quarterly Report on Household Debt and Credit," Federal Reserve Bank of New York, August 2014, http://www.newyorkfed.org/householdcredit/2014-q2/data/pdf/HHDC_2014Q2.pdf.

14 "More than Half of Millennials Say Debt Is Their 'Biggest Financial Concern,' According to Wells Fargo Survey," Wells Fargo, May 22, 2013, https://www.wellsfargo.com/press/2013/20130522_MorethanhalfofMillennials.

15 Donghoon Lee, "Household Debt and Credit: Student Debt."

16 Meta Brown, "Student Debt Overview," Postsecondary National Policy Institute, Federal Reserve Bank of New York, August 14, 2013, http://www.newyorkfed.org/regional/Brown_presentation_GWU_2013Q2.pdf.

17 "Consumer Price Index—November 2014," Bureau of Labor Statistics, January 2015, http://www.bls.gov/news.release/pdf/cpi.pdf.

18 Nicholas Turner, "Who Benefits from Student Aid? The Economic Incidence of Tax-Based Federal Student Aid," *Economics of Education Review* 31, no. 4 (August 2012), pp. 463–481, http://www.sciencedirect.com/science/article/pii/S0272775711001968.

19 Andrew Gillen, "Introducing Bennett Hypothesis 2.0," Center for College Affordability and Productivity, February 2012, http://centerforcollegeaffordability.org/uploads/Introducing _Bennett_Hypothesis_2.pdf.

20 John W. Curtis and Saranna Thornton, "Losing Focus: The Annual Report on the Economic Status of the Profession, 2013–2014," *Academe*, March–April 2014, American Association of University Professors, http://www.aaup.org/file/zreport.pdf.

21 Donna M. Desrochers, Colleen M. Lenihan, and Jane V. Wellman, "Trends in College Spending: 1998–2008," Delta Cost Project, 2010, http://www.deltacostproject.org/sites/ default/files/products/Trends-in-College-Spending-98-08.pdf.

22 "Executive Compensation at Private Colleges, 2012," *Chronicle of Higher Education*, December 8, 2014, http://chronicle.com/factfile/private-ec-2014#id=table.

23 "Executive Compensation at Public Colleges, 2013 Fiscal Year," *Chronicle of Higher Education*, May 16, 2014, http://chronicle.com/article/Executive-Compensation-at /146519/#id=table.

24 Brian Zink, "Purdue Trustees Establish Metrics for Daniels' At-Risk Pay," Purdue University, September 27, 2013, http://www.purdue.edu/newsroom/releases/2013/Q3 /purdue-trustees-establish-metrics-for-daniels-at-risk-pay.html.

25 Curtis and Thornton, "Losing Focus."

26 "Trends in Spending and Institutional Funding: Football Bowl Subdivision (FBS)," Knight Commission on Intercollegiate Athletics, http://spendingdatabase.knightcommission.org /fbs#!quicktabs-tab-division_conferences_and_institu-0.

27 Curtis and Thornton, "Losing Focus."

28 "College: Finances," *USA Today,* accessed August 8, 2014, http://www.usatoday.com/sports /college/schools/finances/.

29 Madeline Stone, "Ten College Dorms with Awesome Amenities," *Business Insider,* October 25, 2013, http://www.businessinsider.com/10-college-dorms-with-awesome-amenities- 2013-10?op=1.

30 "Table 326.10. Graduation Rates of First-Time, Full-Time Bachelor's Degree-Seeking Students at 4-Year Postsecondary Institutions," National Center for Education Statistics, U.S. Department of Education, January 2014, http://nces.ed.gov/programs/digest/d13 /tables/dt13_326.10.asp.

31 Isabel V. Sawhill and Stephanie Owen, "Should Everyone Go to College?" Brookings Institution, May 8, 2013, http://www.brookings.edu/research/interactives/2013 /college-return-on-investment-sawhill.

32 Abel, Deitz, and Su, "Are Recent College Graduates Finding Good Jobs?"

33 Richard Vedder, Christopher Denhart, and Jonathan Robe, "Why Are Recent College Graduates Underemployed?" Center for College Affordability and Productivity, January 2013, http://centerforcollegeaffordability.org/uploads/Underemployed%20Report%202.pdf.

34 "Table 318.20. Bachelor's, Master's, and Doctor's Degrees Conferred by Postsecondary Institutions, by Field of Study: Selected Years, 1970–71 through 2011–12," National Center for Education Statistics, U.S. Department of Education, accessed August 8, 2014, http:// nces.ed.gov/programs/digest/d13/tables/dt13_318.20.asp.

35 "Table 322.10. Bachelor's Degrees Conferred by Postsecondary Institutions, by Field of Study: Selected Years, 1970–71 through 2011–12," National Center for Education Statistics, U.S. Department of Education, accessed August 8, 2014, http://nces.ed.gov/programs /digest/d13/tables/dt13_322.10.asp.

36 "Employment Projections—2012–2022," Bureau of Labor Statistics, December 29, 2013, http://www.bls.gov/news.release/pdf/ecopro.pdf.

37 Diana Furchtgott-Roth, Louis Jacobson, and Christine Mokher, "Strengthening Community Colleges' Influence on Economic Mobility," Pew Charitable Trusts Economic Mobility Project, October 2009, http://www.cna.org/sites/default/files/research/pew_emp _community_colleges.pdf.

38 "Employment Projections: 2012–2022 Summary," Bureau of Labor Statistics, December 19, 2013, http://www.bls.gov/news.release/ecopro.nro.htm.

39 "Trends in College Pricing 2013," College Board, Trends in Higher Education Series, 2013, https://trends.collegeboard.org/sites/default/files/college-pricing-2013-full-report-140108 .pdf.

40 "World University Rankings, 2014–2015," *Times Higher Education*, 2014, http:// www.timeshighereducation.co.uk/world-university-rankings/2014-15/world-ranking.

Chapter 5: Licensing Requirements Keep Out the Young

1 *"Kalish v. Milliken*: Challenging Virginia's Unconstitutional Regulation of Yoga Teacher Training," Institute for Justice, March 10, 2010, http://ij.org/kalish-v-milliken.

2 *"Waugh v. Nevada State Board of Cosmetology*: Nevada Makeup Artists Fight for Their Right to Teach," Institute of Justice, June 19, 2012, http://ij.org/nevadamakeup.

3 "New Texas Law Limits Computer Repair to Licensed Private Investigators: *Rife v. Texas Private Security Board*," Institute for Justice, October 31, 2008, http://ij.org /rife-v-texas-private-security-board-economic-liberty.

4 "Tour Guides in Savannah Sue to End City's Licensing Requirement," Institute for Justice, November 18, 2014, http://ij.org/savannah-nola-tour-guides-free-speech-release-11-18 2014.

5 "IJ Helps Teenager Beat Arizona's Bureaucrats," Institute for Justice, April 28, 2004, https:// www.ij.org/ij-helps-teenager-beat-arizonas-bureaucrats.

6 Dick M. Carpenter II et al., "License to Work: A National Study of Burdens from Occupational Licensing," Institute for Justice, May 2012, p. 16, https://www.ij.org /licensetowork.

7 "U.S. Beer Sales 2013," National Beer Sales & Production Data, Brewers Association, 2013, http://www.brewersassociation.org/statistics/national-beer-sales-production-data/.

8 "Beer Industry Economic Impact in United States," Beer Institute and National Beer Wholesalers Association, 2013, http://www.beerinstitute.org/assets/map-pdfs /Beer_Economic_Impact_US.pdf.

9 "Days to Process Permits Online Original Applications," Alcohol and Tobacco Tax and Trade Bureau, accessed December 9, 2014, http://www.ttb.gov/nrc/average-days.shtml.

10 "Processing Times for Beverage Alcohol Formulas," Alcohol and Tobacco Tax and Trade Bureau, accessed December 9, 2014, http://www.ttb.gov/formulation/processing-times .shtml.

11 "Processing Times for Label Applications," Alcohol and Tobacco Tax and Trade Bureau, accessed December 9, 2014, http://www.ttb.gov/labeling/processing-times.shtml.

12 Matthew Mitchell and Christopher Koopman, "Bottling Up Innovation in Craft Brewing: A Review of the Current Barriers and Challenges," Mercatus Center at George Mason University, June 2014, http://mercatus.org/sites/default/files/MitchellKoopman-CraftBrewing-MOP.pdf.

13 VA Code Ann. § 4.1-222, 2014, https://leg1.state.va.us/cgi-bin/legp504 .exe?000+cod+4.1-222.

14 Morris M. Kleiner and Alan B. Krueger, "Analyzing the Extent and Influence of Occupational Licensing on the Labor Market," *Journal of Labor Economics* 31, no. 2 (April 2013), pp. 173–202.

15 Carpenter et al., "License to Work: A National Study," pp. 4–5.

16 Ibid., p. 11.

17 Ibid., pp. 93, 136.

18 Ibid., p. 12.

19 Ibid., p. 13.

20 Dick M. Carpenter II, "Testing the Utility of Licensing: Evidence from a Field Experiment on Occupational Regulation," *Journal of Applied Business and Economics* 13, no. 2 (2012), pp. 28–41, http://m.www.na-businesspress.com/JABE/CarpenterDM_Web13_2_.pdf.

21 "Unemployment Rates for States," Bureau of Labor Statistics, June 2014, http://www.bls .gov/web/laus/laumstrk.htm.

22 "Small Business Friendliness Survey," Thumbtack.com and the Kauffman Foundation, June 2014, http://www.thumbtack.com/survey#/2014/1/states.

23 Jon Lieber and Sander Daniels, "2014 Thumbtack.com Small Business Friendliness Survey: Methodology & Analysis," Thumback.com, June 2014, p. 9, http://heartland.org/sites /default/files/friendliness_2014.pdf.

24 Ibid., p. 11.

25 Ibid., p. 10.

26 Ibid., pp. 26–27.

27 "Widespread but Slower Growth in 2013," Bureau of Economic Analysis, June 11, 2014, http://www.bea.gov/newsreleases/regional/gdp_state/gsp_newsrelease.htm.

28 Lieber and Daniels, "2014 Thumbtack.com Small Business Friendliness Survey," p. 1.

29 Ian Hathaway and Robert E. Litan, "The Other Aging of America: The Increasing Dominance of Older Firms," Brookings Institution, July 31, 2014, http://www.brookings.edu /research/papers/2014/07/aging-america-increasing-dominance-older-firms-litan.

30 John Dearie and Courtney Geduldig, *Where the Jobs Are: Entrepreneurship and the Soul of the American Economy* (Hoboken, NJ: John Wiley and Sons, 2013).

31 John Dearie and Courtney Geduldig, "Entrepreneurship and the Soul of the American Economy," Economics21, Manhattan Institute for Policy Research, November 11, 2013, http://www.economics21.org/commentary/entrepreneurship-and-soul-american-economy.

32 Robert J. Thornton and Edward J. Timmons, "Licensing One of the World's Oldest Professions: Massage," *Journal of Law and Economics* 56, no. 2 (May 2013), pp. 371–388.

33 Sidney L Carroll and Robert J. Gaston, "Occupational Restrictions and the Quality of Service Received: Some Evidence," *Southern Economic Journal* 47, no. 4 (April 1981), pp. 959–976.

34 Jonathan V. Hall and Alan B. Krueger, "An Analysis of the Labor Market for Uber's Driver-Partners in the United States," January 22, 2015, https://s3.amazonaws.com/uber-static /comms/PDF/Uber_Driver-Partners_Hall_Kreuger_2015.pdf.

35 "Motor Vehicle Accidents—Number and Deaths: 1990 to 2009," U.S. Census Bureau, 2012, https://www.census.gov/compendia/statab/2012/tables/12s1103.pdf.

36 Sean M. Malone, *Locked Out: A Mississippi Success Story*, Honest Enterprise, April 2014.

37 Dick M. Carpenter II and John K. Ross, "The Power of One Entrepreneur: Melony Armstrong," Institute for Justice, October 2009, http://ij.org/melony-artmstrong.

Chapter 6: Banned from the Job Market

1 "Wage and Salary Workers Paid Hourly Rates with Earnings at or below the Prevailing Federal Minimum Wage by Selected Characteristics," Bureau of Labor Statistics, 2014, http://www.bls.gov/cps/cpsaat44.pdf.

2 "Chili's and Ziosk Complete Installation of Largest Tabletop Tablet Network in the U.S.," Yahoo! Finance, June 9, 2014, http://finance.yahoo.com/news/chilis-ziosk-complete-installation-largest-150000331.html.

3 "Employment Status of the Civilian Population by Race, Sex, and Age," Bureau of Labor Statistics, January 2015, http://www.bls.gov/news.release/empsit.to2.htm.

4 "Current Population Survey," Bureau of Labor Statistics, January 2015.

5 Ibid.

6 "School Enrollment, CPS October 2003 Through 2012—Detailed Tables," United States Census Bureau, 2013.

7 "Wage and Salary Workers Paid Hourly Rates with Earnings at or below the Prevailing Federal Minimum Wage by Selected Characteristics," Bureau of Labor Statistics, 2014, http://www.bls.gov/cps/cpsaat44.pdf.

8 Eric Schlosser, *Fast Food Nation: The Dark Side of the All-American Meal* (Boston: Houghton Mifflin, 2000), pp. 4, 282.

9 James Sherk, "What Is Minimum Wage: Its History and Effects on the Economy: Testimony Before the Health, Education, Labor, and Pensions Committee, United States Senate," Heritage Foundation, June 25, 2013, http://www.heritage.org/research/testimony/2013/06 /what-is-minimum-wage-its-history-and-effects-on-the-economy#_ftnref9.

10 Arindrajit Dube, T. William Lester, and Michael Reich, "Minimum Wage Effects Across State Borders: Estimates Using Contiguous Counties," *Review of Economics and Statistics* 92, no. 4 (November 2010), pp. 945–964, http://www.mitpressjournals.org/doi/abs/10.1162 /REST_a_00039#.U863TvldXz4.

11 David Neumark, J.M. Ian Salas, and William Wascher, "Revisiting the Minimum Wage-Employment Debate: Throwing Out the Baby with the Bathwater?" Institute for the Study of Labor, July 2013, http://www.socsci.uci.edu/~dneumark/Neumark%20et%20al%20 MW%20evaluation%20May%202013%20ILRR%20final%20rev.pdf.

12 Vernon Smith et al., "A Statement to Federal Policymakers," March 2014, http://nebula .wsimg.com/faf44fea2172ad008b46a64835ae2492?AccessKeyId=D2418B43C2D698C15401& disposition=0&alloworigin=1.

13 Jonathan Meer and Jeremy West, "Effects of the Minimum Wage on Employment Dynamics," Texas A&M University, December 2013, http://econweb.tamu.edu/jmeer /Meer_West_Minimum_Wage.pdf.

14 David Neumark and William L. Wascher, "Minimum Wages and Employment," *Foundations and Trends in Microeconomics* 3, no. 1–2 (2007), http://www.socsci.uci .edu/~dneumark/min_wage_review.pdf.

15 Ibid.

16 "Average Hourly and Weekly Earnings of Production and Nonsupervisory Employees on Private Nonfarm Payrolls by Industry Sector, Seasonally Adjusted," Bureau of Labor Statistics, January 2015, http://www.bls.gov/news.release/empsit.t24.htm.

17 "The Effects of a Minimum-Wage Increase on Employment and Family Income," Congressional Budget Office, February 18, 2014, http://www.cbo.gov/publication/44995.

18 "Form LM-2 Labor Organization Annual Report," United Food and Commercial Workers International Union, U.S. Department of Labor, March 26, 2014.

19 "May 2013 Occupational Employment and Wages: Waiters and Waitresses," Bureau of Labor Statistics, April 1, 2014, http://www.bls.gov/oes/current/oes353031.htm.

20 "May 2013 Metropolitan and Nonmetropolitan Area Occupational Employment and Wage Estimates," Bureau of Labor Statistics, April 1, 2014, http://www.bls.gov/oes/current /oessrcma.htm.

21 "Consolidated State Minimum Wage Update Table," Department of Labor, January 1, 2015, http://www.dol.gov/whd/minwage/america.htm.

22 Ibid.

23 "State Minimum Wages," National Conference of State Legislatures, December 9, 2014, http://www.ncsl.org/research/labor-and-employment/state-minimum-wage-chart.aspx.

24 "Cost of Living Data Series, Third Quarter 2014," Missouri Economic Research and Information Center, http://www.missourieconomy.org/indicators/cost_of_living/.

25 "May 2013 State Occupational Employment and Wage Estimates," Bureau of Labor Statistics, April 1, 2014, http://www.bls.gov/oes/current/oessrcst.htm.

26 "Impact of Increased Minimum Wage of American Samoa & CNMI," hearing before the Committee of Energy and Natural Resources, United States Senate, February 28, 2008, http://www.gpo.gov/fdsys/pkg/CHRG-110shrg42474/html/CHRG-110shrg42474.htm.

27 "May 2013 State Occupational Employment and Wage Estimates," Bureau of Labor Statistics, April 1, 2014, http://www.bls.gov/oes/current/oessrcst.htm.

28 "Maximum Hypocrisy on the Minimum Wage," Employment Policies Institute, January 27, 2014, http://www.minimumwage.com/2014/01/maximum-hypocrisy-on-the-minimum-wage/.

29 "Internship Programs Under the Fair Labor Standards Act," U.S. Department of Labor Wage and Hour Division, April 2010, http://www.dol.gov/whd/regs/compliance/whdfs71.pdf.

30 "*Musallam v. CBS Broadcasting, Inc.*," Supreme Court of the State of New York, September 4, 2014, https://pmcdeadline2.files.wordpress.com/2014/09/cbs-letterman-interns-class-action-sept-4-2014.pdf.

31 "Undergraduate Tuition," George Washington University, accessed August 6, 2014, http://studentaccounts.gwu.edu/undergraduate-tuition.

32 "College Costs: FAQs," College Board, accessed December 10, 2014, https://bigfuture.collegeboard.org/pay-for-college/college-costs/college-costs-faqs.

33 John M. Nunley et al., "College Major, Internship Experience, and Employment Opportunities: Estimates from a Résumé Audit" (working paper series, Auburn University Department of Economics, March 30, 2014), http://cla.auburn.edu/econwp/archives/2014/2014-03.pdf.

34 Brett Arends, "How Summer Can Change Your Future," *Wall Street Journal*, May 16, 2014, http://online.wsj.com/news/articles/SB10001424052702303851804579560000701747102.

35 "May 2013 Metropolitan and Nonmetropolitan Area Occupational Employment and Wage Estimates: Seattle-Tacoma-Bellevue, WA Metropolitan Division," Bureau of Labor Statistics, April 1, 2014, http://www.bls.gov/oes/current/oes_42660.htm.

36 "May 2013 Metropolitan and Nonmetropolitan Area Occupational Employment and Wage Estimates: San Francisco-San Mateo-Redwood City, CA Metropolitan Division," Bureau of Labor Statistics, April 1, 2014, http://www.bls.gov/oes/current/oes_41884.htm.

37 "Increasing the Minimum Wage: Economic Impact Report," Office of Economic Analysis, Office of the Controller, City and County of San Francisco, July 17, 2014, http://sfcontroller.org/Modules/ShowDocument.aspx?documentid=5495.

38 "Cost of Living Index—Selected Urban Areas, Annual Average: 2010," U.S. Census Bureau, 2012, http://www.census.gov/compendia/statab/2012/tables/12s0728.pdf.

39 "May 2013 Metropolitan and Nonmetropolitan Area Occupational Employment and Wage Estimates: Seattle-Bellevue-Everett, WA Metropolitan Division," Bureau of Labor Statistics, April 1, 2014, http://www.bls.gov/oes/current/oes_42644.htm.

40 "May 2013 Metropolitan and Nonmetropolitan Area Occupational Employment and Wage Estimates: Myrtle Beach-North Myrtle Beach-Conway, SC Metropolitan Division," Bureau of Labor Statistics, April 1, 2014, http://www.bls.gov/oes/current/oes_34820.htm.

Chapter 7: Reclaiming the Disinherited Generation

1 "AARP Profile," Open Secrets, Center for Responsive Politics, accessed November 26, 2014, https://www.opensecrets.org/orgs/summary.php?id=D000023726&cycle=2014.

2 "National Cmte to Preserve Social Security & Medicare Profile," Open Secrets, Center for Responsive Politics, accessed August 20, 2014, https://www.opensecrets.org/orgs/summary.php?id=D000000142&cycle=2012.

3 Thom File, "Young-Adult Voting: An Analysis of Presidential Elections, 1964–2012," U.S. Census Bureau, April 2014, http://www.census.gov/prod/2014pubs/p20-573.pdf.

4 "Millennials: The Politically Unclaimed Generation," Reason-Rupe Spring 2014 Millennial Survey, http://reason.com/assets/db/2014-millennials-report.pdf.

5 "Code of Federal Regulations Page Breakdown—1975 through 2013," Office of the Federal Register, 2014, https://www.federalregister.gov/uploads/2014/04 /CFR-Actual-Pages-published1-2013.pdf.

6 "Regdata: Historical Regulation Data," Mercatus Center at George Mason University, accessed November 26, 2014, http://regdata.org/index.php?type=regulatory _restrictions&regulator[]=0.

7 John W. Dawson and John J. Seater, "Federal Regulation and Aggregate Economic Growth," *Journal of Economic Growth* 18, no. 2 (June 2013), pp. 137–77, http://link.springer.com /article/10.1007%252Fs10887-013-9088-y.

8 Norman Loayza, Ana Maria Oviedo, and Luis Serven, "The Impact of Regulation on Growth and Informality," World Bank, May 2005, http://elibrary.worldbank.org/doi /pdf/10.1596/1813-9450-3623.

9 Diana Thomas, "Regressive Effects of Regulation," Mercatus Center, November 2012, http:// mercatus.org/sites/default/files/RegressiveEffects_Thomas_v1-0.pdf.

10 "2014 Annual Report," Board of Trustees, Federal Old-Age and Survivors Insurance and Federal Disability Insurance Trust Funds," July 28, 2014, http://www.ssa.gov/oact/tr/2014 /tr2014.pdf.

11 Steuerle, *Dead Men Ruling*.

Chapter 8: Conclusion

1 Christopher DeMuth, "Our Democratic Debt," *National Review*, July 21, 2014, http://www .nationalreview.com/article/392771/our-democratic-debt-chris-demuth.

INDEX

Tables are indicated by *italicized* page numbers.